Why Is There
a
New Testament?

Background Books 5

Why Is There
a
New Testament?

by

Joseph F. Kelly

 **Michael Glazier**
Wilmington, Delaware

About the Author

Joseph F. Kelly is Professor of New Testament and Early Christianity at John Carroll University. He received his doctorate from Fordham University and is a specialist in the history of biblical interpretation. His publications include a volume in the *Corpus Christianorum* series and many articles in European and American journals, including *Vigiliae Christianae, Revue Bénédictine,* and *Studia Patristica,* as well as in popular journals such as *Emmanuel* and *The Bible Today.*

The publisher wishes to thank and to acknowledge the following for the illustrations used in this book: Library of Congress, page 27; Deutches Archaeologisches Institut, page 35; Pacific School of Religion, page 126; Biblioteca Apostolic Vatican, page 128; British Museum, page 131; Laurentian Library, page 159; The Pontifico Istituto di Archeologia Christiana, pages 180, 182 and 184.

First published in *Background Books* in 1986 by Michael Glazier, Inc., 1935 West Fourth Street, Wilmington, Delaware, 19805.

CONTENTS

Preface 11

Abbreviations 14

1. Our Understanding of the New Testament 15

2. The Composition of the New Testament Books to the
   Death of Apostle Paul 21
   A. The First Writings 24
   B. The Pauline Epistles 29
   C. The Neronian Persecution 34
   D. The Jewish War 36

3. The Second Generation and Later 38
   I. The Gospels 38
   A. Oral Traditions 39
   B. Mark 42
   C. Oral Tradition after Mark.............. 44
   D. Luke 45
   E. Matthew 47
   F. John 52
   II. The Later Books of the New Testament...... 55
   A. The Pastorals 55
   B. The Johannine Epistles 56
   C. Peter, James, and Jude 57
   D. Ephesians............................ 60
   E. Hebrews 61
   F. Revelation 62
   G. Acts................................. 64

5

4. From Books to Testament: The Canon........... 68
   I. The New Testament Evidence 69
     A. The Earliest Authorities 69
     B. Paul................................... 71
     C. The Gospels 74
     D. Revelation and the Non-Pauline Epistles .. 75
   II. The Patristic Evidence.................... 78
     A. Scripture and Patristics 78
     B. The Earliest Fathers 80
     C. The Apologists 86
     D. Marcion 87
     E. Montanus.............................. 89
     F. Apostolicity and Gnosticism 91
     G. Irenaeus of Lyons...................... 92
     H. Which Books?......................... 96
     I. The Alexandrians 98
     J. The Closing of the Canon 101

5. The New Testament Apocryphal Books 103
     A. Gospels............................... 107
     B. Epistles 111
     C. Acts.................................. 112
     D. Apocalypses.......................... 116
     E. The Apocrypha and the Canon.......... 117

6. What the New Testament Says................. 120
     A. Textual Criticism 124
     B. How Books Were Produced 125
     C. Who Made the Surviving Copies? 129
     D. Evaluating the Evidence 133

7. "Teach Ye All Nations" 141
   I. The Value of the Translations 142
   II. The Eastern Versions...................... 145
     A. Syriac Versions 145
     B. Coptic Versions 147
     C. The Armenian Version................. 149
     D. Other Eastern Versions 151
     E. The African Versions 153
   III. The Western Versions 154
     A. The Latin Versions.................... 154

B. The Gothic Version.................... 160
C. Later Western Versions 162

8. Spirituality and Art 164
   I.Spirituality 165
   A. Martyrdom 165
     1. Martyrdom in the New Testament... 166
     2. Polycarp 167
     3. The Martyrs of Lyons 168
     4. Perpetua and Felicity 169
     5. Pionius 170
   B. Monasticism........................ 171
     1. The Beginnings of Monasticism 172
     2. Monastic Literature and the
       New Testament 173
   II.Early Christian Art 175
   A. Iconography 175
   B. The Earliest Art 176
   C. New Testament Themes 178
   D. The Next Generations 182

Bibliography.................................... 186

Glossary 191

Index 195

Ellen, uxori amatae meae
". . . tu supergressa es universas" (Prov 31:29)

PREFACE

Like many books written for a non-specialist audience, this one began in a classroom. I was teaching a course on the New Testament and one day asked the students, "If you were at an Early Christian liturgy and someone was reading from a gospel book, what would that book look like?" No one knew, so I explained the difference between a roll and a codex. To my delight, the students were quite interested, so I began to devote more and more class time to non-exegetical matters, such as the canon and the apocrypha. Soon I was teaching a separate course entitled "The Bible in the Early Church," which gave rise to this book.

This book, like that course, is intended to meet a need. New Testament classes rightly concentrate on exegesis, and because of the vast amount of material just on that, teachers often do not have the opportunity to spend time on other matters relating to the New Testament. Furthermore, there is no convenient book to use to cover these. But students will still ask questions about why there are just twenty-seven books in the New Testament or about how we can be sure that we know exactly what Paul or Luke wrote. In this book I have tried to explain matters like the text and the canon clearly and concisely and, more importantly, to provide a setting for a better understanding of the exegesis. My thesis throughout is that the earliest communities produced the

New Testament, and I have tried to relate all my individual topics to the life of the early Church.

Many aspects of the New Testament present problems to both scholar and layman, for example, the dates of the biblical books or the exact number of Pauline epistles. This book makes no pretense at solving all the knotty problems. In general, I have tried to present a moderate view based upon the current consensus of scholars, where that consensus exists. Where it does not exist, I have made a judgment based upon my reading of the evidence, for example, on the importance of Marcion for the New Testament canon. Naturally some will disagree with my conclusions; to them I can only say that in a more specialized book I could have given some matters a more thorough and nuanced treatment, and I must ask their indulgence.

This book was written with a word-processing program on the John Carroll University main-frame computer. It was my first such effort, and I often needed and received assistance, which I am glad to acknowledge. My thanks to Mr. Donald Grazko, director of the university computer center, and his assistants, Susan Ziemianski, Robert Gilliland, and Robert Kozel; to Rev. Roy Drake, S.J., director of institutional planning and his assistants, Maura Sweeney and Lawrence Van Wie, who arranged time for me to use the university's letter-quality printer; to Dr. Carl Spitznagel of the mathematics department who offered a mini-course on word-processing which helped me greatly.

Research time for this book and regular reduced teaching loads were provided by the university committee on research and service; my thanks to the members of the committee and its chairman, Dr. Louis Pecek, as well as to my department chairman, Rev. Kevin O'Connell, S.J., who warmly recommended me to the committee for that research time.

My scholarly specialty is the history of exegesis. Three foundations, the American Council of Learned Societies, the American Philosophical Society, and the National Endowment for the Humanities, have provided me various types of generous assistance to pursue research in that field.

In the course of that research, I came across much material which aided me in the writing of this book, so I wish to thank those foundations for their indirect but valuable aid.

Finally, let me thank my wife Ellen who provided me with support, encouragement, and, most of all, free time to write. This book is gratefully dedicated to her.

Abbreviations

The abbreviations of the New Testament books are those used in most modern bibles, for example, 1 Cor for 1 Corinthians. I just note three other abbreviations which appear in the book:

RSV - the Revised Standard Version, a modern American translation of the Bible.

NTM - New Testament Message, a series of commentaries upon which I often relied for the dates and places of the biblical books.

Eusebius, *H. E.* - the *Historia Ecclesiastica*, or *History of the Church* by Eusebius, bishop of Caesarea (died *circa* 339), the basic non-scriptural source for the history of Christianity in the first three centuries.

1

OUR UNDERSTANDING OF THE NEW TESTAMENT

This book is about how the New Testament came into being in the life of the early Church. At first this may seem superfluous because there are so many reliable general accounts available on the formation of the gospels, the career of Paul, and the so-called 'lesser' books, such as the Catholic Epistles (1-3 John, 1-2 Peter, James, Jude). But how the New Testament books came to be differs considerably from how the New Testament came to be.

Think of what we mean by the words "New Testament." We mean a collection of twenty-seven books - no more or less - which Christians consider to be somehow inspired by God and to contain a divine message for us about our beliefs and practices. We further recognize these books to be complementary with and equal to the Hebrew Scriptures, that is, the Christian Old Testament, and to deserve equal authority and reverence. These books always appear in a certain order, for example, the gospels in the sequence of Matthew, Mark, Luke, and John, and the books are divided into chapters and verses. The content of the New Testament is set, and no true Christian would tamper with its works or wording. Finally, although these books are individual entities, they are not completely separated ones, that is, they belong to a greater whole.

The foregoing is a general and intentionally non-controversial description. Many authors would add much more, such as the New Testament is a radical challenge to our being or it is a blueprint for Christ's imminent second coming to this morally decadent world; here I have stuck to elements with which all Christians could agree. Yet basic and general as these observations may be, they have not been true of every period of church history and *not one* of them is true of the age when the New Testament books were being written or shortly thereafter, that is, until *circa* 150.

One might object that of course none of those things could be true while the New Testament was still being composed and until the last book, 2 Peter, was written around 125, but we must realize that the New Testament is more than just the books. It is also an attitude and an understanding about those books; if the notion of New Testament did not exist, the books would be simply twenty-seven independent works. Let me illustrate this with the most basic point, the name "New Testament." (I say that is the most basic point because before we have even read one word, we have seen the title, and it conveys a message to us.) There would be no "new" testament unless there were an "old" one. But nowhere in the "new" is there any concept of an "old" one. The New Testament writers refer and allude constantly to the Hebrew Scriptures, and they refer to them with a variety of terms such as Scripture, the Law, the Law and the prophets, or "it is written," but nowhere do they refer to an "old" testament of inspired books. There is simply no conception of a new set of Christian books understood as scripture and complementary to the now Old Testament. To the early Christians, the Hebrew scriptures were simply scripture, "inspired by God and profitable for teaching, reproof, for correction, and for training in righteousness." (2 Timothy 3:16; RSV). Later generations would recognize a set of Christian scriptures and call them a "new" testament to distinguish them from the Hebrew scriptures, which were then relegated to being "old," a distinction which has too often proved to be a division.

[The Greek term for New Testament is *kaine diatheke*, literally, "new covenant." That phrase appears several times in the New Testament, for example, Luke 22:20, 1 Corinthians 11:25, 2 Corinthians 3:6, Hebrews 8:8, 9:15. The term also appears in the Old Testament, in Jeremiah. 31:31, and Hebrews 8:8 uses it when quoting Jeremiah. 2 Corinthians 3:14 uses the phrase "old covenant," and Galatians 4:24 speaks of "two covenants." All these uses, however, refer to a covenant and not to a fixed collection of books.]

Let me give a few more examples. All Christian denominations accept a New Testament of twenty-seven books, yet nowhere in the New Testament is there a list of those books. The canon, or formal list of books, is a product of the second century, and *it is not until the year 367* that any Christian writer knows a New Testament consisting of those twenty-seven. The Christian will rightly believe that these twenty-seven were always inspired even if that inspiration was not recognized immediately, but the development of the canon proves that a most basic and crucial element in our understanding of the New Testament, namely, what books belong in it, was a product of the post-apostolic age and had little relevance to the people who wrote or received the inspired books. (Older generations of biblical fundamentalists, who were dreadfully worried that the Bible might owe anything to the Church, used to say that the character or nature of the books made it clear that they were inspired. This is fine to say, but if it is true, we must be amazed at the obtuseness of the early Christians who needed two-and-a-half centuries after the composition of the last New Testament book to recognize which ones were inspired.)

Since all the books belong to the New Testament, we modern Christians see an underlying unity, but this perception is also a product of the post-apostolic age. Indeed, several scriptural authors would have had trouble recognizing this unity since they occasionally set out to correct one another, for example, James 2:14-23 on Romans 4:1-25 or 2 Peter 2:1-22 on Jude 5-16. And does the book of Revelation, with its emphasis on vengeance and its absence of mercy, agree that well with the teaching of Jesus as presented in the gospels? As a Christian, I accept the New Testament's basic unity, but as an historian I must point out that this unity was not apparent to some of the scriptural writers.

We see all the books as inspired, but did anyone who wrote an inspired book see it that way? The author of Revelation apparently did, but no one else. Paul had a strong sense of his apostolic authority and thought that his letters carried this authority, but authority and inspiration are far different concepts. And did the author of 2 and 3 John really consider his little letters to be Scripture in the same sense that Isaiah and Exodus were? Let me quote the English scholar, C. F. D. Moule:

> But he (Paul) cannot have written them (his epistles) with the faintest notion that they would become 'scripture' or even be preserved for long. (*Understanding the New Testament*, p. 86).

His words can be applied equally well to the other Christian authors.

Although most Christians know the New Testament in a variety of translations (Revised Standard Version, Jerusalem Bible, New English Bible), they presume that all the individual translations are based upon the text of the books as they were written in the original language (Greek) by the original writers. Furthermore, this original text is so sacred that no Christian would dare to alter it and certainly not to propagate his or her own ideas. But the fact is that we do not have the "original" text of a single New Testament book, only copies made a century or more later, and as for altering the text, this was frequently done to Mark's gospel by Luke and Matthew, and various early Christian groups returned the favor to those gospels. The Greek text of the New Testament is a product of the early Church, and so is our reverence for that text.

These examples will be developed and studied in later chapters, but I hope they have demonstrated that the New

Testament as we know it and, more importantly, as we understand it, was a product of the post-apostolic age or, more accurately, the early Church, here understood as the period from the time of the apostles to the fourth century when Christianity changed from an occasionally oppressed minority sect to the offical religion of the state. We will investigate the rise of the New Testament in the life of the whole Church, of the Christian people. This emphasis on the community in no way lessens the originality - indeed, the genius - of the evangelists or other Early Christian writers. On the contrary, their matchless contribution, so well discussed in other books, will be taken for granted. This book will simply look at the writings, even the most technical, from another point of view, that of the community from whom these people wrote.

Before going further, I should explain how I will understand the term "community." In his book *The Myth of Christian Beginnings*, Robert Wilken has shown how later generations of Christians idealized the earliest age and the earliest community. Too many of us have taken too literally Luke's description of it in Acts 2:42 and 4:32. "And they devoted themselves to the apostles' teaching and fellowship, to the breaking of bread and prayers." "Now the company of those who believed were of one heart and soul,..." Anytime we find ourselves rhapsodizing about the Acts community, we should quickly turn to the fractious, bibulous, incestuous Christians of 1 Corinthians 1-8 to balance the view. Although it would be mistaken to view Corinth as a typical community of the day, it would be even more mistaken to view the Acts community as typical. There never was an ideal community because every community is made up of sinners. To idealize a group is effectively to make it unreal and thus irrelevant. What meaning can a perfect community like that have for a community of sinners like us? How much more meaningful to us is a story like that of St. Augustine who sinned as much we do and probably more, but who strove to be a better Christian and finally succeeded. Or we can imitate Martin Luther, overwhelmed by the sense of his own sinfulness and tortured by self-doubt about the rightness of his cause, but always trusting to God's will and grace.

In fairness to the early Christians, we must abandon an idealization of them and see them as much like ourselves - sinners who are always trying to do better, always failing, always trying again, and all the time counting on God's help. Our Christian ancestors did not go about all day praying and meditating on the nature of God or discussing theological problems. They had to work for a living in a harsher society and under worse conditions than we know. They worried about money, were jealous of those who did better, took pride in their children's successes, bet on sporting events, were titillated by the scandals of the imperial court, and complained about governments and politics. And they were Christians, too. They did pray and meditate when they could, and they took an interest in theological discussions, if they could follow them. In a world of unbelievers, they helped to spread the faith. In times of persecution, a remarkable number stood fast, although, inevitably in a community of sinners, some apostasized rather than suffer. Some of these Christians came late to the liturgies; some were reluctant to contribute to the needs of the community; some even fell asleep during sermons (once with a temporarily fatal result; cf. Acts 20:7-12). Some were saints; all were sinners. Some were leaders; most were followers; all were involved. If we modern Christians could travel back in time to the early Church, we would find no golden age but people like ourselves, and they would certainly be amazed and amused to know that their era of short lives, hard work, and fear of persecution was "golden."

Let us see these people as our sisters and brothers in every way, and let us see how their lived experience of Christianity affected the formation of the New Testament.

2

THE COMPOSITION OF THE NEW TESTAMENT BOOKS TO THE DEATH OF APOSTLE PAUL

Christianity is so inextricably linked with the Bible, the Hebrew Scriptures and the New Testament, that we simply cannot imagine it without God's word in written form. It is therefore supremely important and also supremely ironic that Jesus, founder and foundation of Christianity, wrote nothing, although as we shall see later, the Church at Edessa claimed to have a letter of his.

Could Jesus have written? Almost certainly he could. Literary education at least for boys was common in the Judea of his day; village schools were often associated with the local synagogues. We know that Jesus could read (Luke 4:17), and his constant debates with the Pharisees and others about the Scriptures and Pharisaic regulations, for example, Mark 12:10-11, indicate that he was well read in his own traditions. It is unlikely he would have been taught to read without simultaneously having been taught to write. Finally, even if he could not write himself, he could have dictated to a secretary as Paul did. We are left with the inescapable conclusion that Jesus deliberately chose not to commit his message to writing.

At first sight this seems strange for a religious teacher who belonged to the "People of the Book" as the Prophet Mohammed called the Jews. On the other hand, this is not an unknown phenomenon for great teachers in ancient, literate societies. For example, the Buddha, Zoroaster, Lao-Tse, Confucius, Socrates, and the Teacher of Righteousness at Qumran apparently did not write down their teachings. We know of them through what their disciples or even much later writers chose to preserve. In fact, the third-century A.D. Persian religious leader Mani claimed that the teachings of Buddha, Zoroaster, and Jesus were distorted by their disciples and would eventually perish, while he, by writing books, would create a religion which would last until the end of time. (Great religious teachers need not be great prognosticators.)

A second explanation may be found in the eschatological nature of earliest Christianity, that is, it emphasized an early return of the risen Jesus and the consequent end of the world. We know the Early Christians believed in this; no less than Paul gives indisputable witness to it (1 Thessalonians 4:13-18). But most modern exegetes, including Roman Catholics who were long hesitant on this point, think that Jesus himself believed in an imminent end (cf. Mark 13, esp. v. 30). It may be that Jesus, anticipating only the briefest of missions for himself and his disciples, saw no need to put his message in a permanent form when the world itself had no permanence.

But these explanations are just reasoned conjectures. All we can be certain of is that Jesus left no authentic writings.

After Jesus' death and resurrection, none of his disciples, none of the Twelve, wrote anything about what he did or said. It appears, in fact, that they wrote nothing at all, or at least nothing which has survived. Christian tradition attributed much to them: a gospel to Matthew, two epistles to Peter, an epistle to Jude, another epistle to James (although James, the brother of the Lord, was more frequently thought to be the author), and a gospel, three epistles, and apocalypse to John. The consensus of modern scholars is that not one of those works can be indisputably attributed to a member of the Twelve, and only 1 Peter is considered possible, and then only if "Peter" relied heavily upon his secretary Silvanus (1 Peter 5:12).

Suppose one of the Twelve did write and suppose his work were now discovered, would it not have to be included in the New Testament? First, any writing claiming to be by one of the Twelve would have to pass excruciatingly rigorous tests for authenticity. The works now in the New Testament have been known to the Christian world since the second century, and some of them barely made it into the canon. Any new work would find it almost impossible. Second, even if it were deemed authentic, authorship by one of the Twelve is not equivalent to canonicity. Should everything written by an apostle be in the New Testament? In the fourth chapter we will see what criteria the Early Christians used to determine what books should be in the New Testament, and authorship by one of the Twelve or Paul was not an absolute criterion.

Why did the Twelve not write? Possibly they followed the example of their Master. Possibly they also thought the world would end soon (cf. Acts 1:6) and saw no need for writing. They were not alone in this. Paul probably became a Christian *circa* 36, yet he did not write his first epistle, 1 Thessalonians, until *circa* 50, more than a dozen years later. We can safely assume that his mind was active for all that time, but his pen, so active in later years, was not. The first generation of Christians simply did not commit their teaching to writing. That step resulted from an outside stimulus, the persecution and dispersal recorded in Acts 8.

Until then the Christians lived mostly in Jerusalem, but the persecution forcibly expelled many of them, most likely the "Hellenists," who then carried the Word outside Jerusalem and even to non-Jewish areas. The dispersal of the Christians precipitated the first stage of the central drama of Acts, whether or not Christianity should be opened to non-Jews. The contacts with non-Jews (the Samaritans, the Ethiopian eunuch) raised the question in a practical way, and it soon became a theoretical one, that is, it moved from the pastoral to the theological dimension. At all events, the Twelve, apparently led by Peter, agreed to the admission of Gentiles, although the question of requirements remained (cf. Acts 15). After the (symbolic) account of the conversion of the Roman centurion Cornelius and his family, Luke shifts his attention to the missionary endeavors which effectively made Christianity a lived universal religion.

The problem inherent in Luke's account is his focus on his hero Paul to the virtual exclusion of other missionaries. We know of the work of Paul in the small towns and large cities of Asia Minor and Greece, but what was happening elsewhere? It is historically probable that the first Christian writings, now non-extant, were to or by other, now anonymous missionaries.

A. The First Writings

In Acts Paul follows a deliberate pattern. He goes first to the local synagogue to preach his message to the Jews; after the almost inevitable rejection, he turns his attention to the local pagans. If we accept this general scenario, and there is no reason not to, we face an immediate question. If Christian missionaries went to small towns in Asia Minor because those towns had Jewish residents, why did they not also go to the great city of Alexandria with its large Jewish community? The answer is that missionaries must have gone there, even if we must discount the tradition that the evangelist Mark was the founder of that church (Eusebius, *H.E.* 2, 16). We must also expect that missionaries were sent to the sizeable Jewish community resident in Babylon.

In Acts, Luke says that when missionaries went into a new area, the Jerusalem community wanted to know of their activities and reserved to itself the right of approval. Peter and John went to investigate what was happening in Samaria (Acts 8:14-25), and Paul and Barnabas reported to Jerusalem. We cannot say for certain what type of authority the Jerusalem community exercised over these various missions, but the missionaries and the "home board" recognized the need for contacts. If, as seems historically probable, missionaries went to the Jewish communities in Alexandria and Babylon (and possibly Rome), the contacts with the Jerusalem church would have been maintained. If personal contact were not feasible, letters would have been the obvious answer. This is only a hypothesis, but a reasonable one based on the historical situation, on what Luke tells us of Paul's missionary work, and on the factors which first caused Paul to write.

Let us return to the communities we do know about. The faith spread quickly throughout Judea and then to other areas outside Judea - Samaria (Acts 8), Damascus (Acts 9:2), Phoenicia, Cyprus, and most importantly, Antioch (Acts 11:19). In that great Levantine city the followers of Jesus were first called Christians (Acts 11:26), obviously by pagans because the Greek word *Christos* means "the Christ," "the Messiah," and it is not likely that Jews would have called Jesus' followers "those of the Messiah." This also means that as early as *circa* 36 observant pagans could distinguish the Christians from other Jewish groups.

What would be the consequences for the Christians and for scripture of these contacts with pagans? In recent years scholars have rightly questioned the sharp distinctions previously made between "Palestinian" and "Hellenistic" Christianity; surely there was much overlapping. Furthermore, the existence of Jewish communities around the Mediterranean guaranteed that some of the concepts basic to the Christians, who were mostly Jews, would be somewhat familiar to the pagans. But we must not minimize the differences between Christianity and paganism and the effects those differences had upon the presentation of the Christian message.

For example, we usually think that the major question of Acts, whether Gentiles converts should be bound by Jewish legal regulations, was the major practical issue for the earliest missionaries because of Luke's emphasis. But I suggest that the Old Testament was a far greater problem. The first Christians, almost all Jews, took it for granted. To the

Christians, as to all Jews (Acts 2), the newness of their message was the person of Jesus in whom God had worked. But when an early Christian preacher proclaimed to a group of pagans that Jesus was a man through whom God worked, almost certainly someone would asked, "*Which* God?" And, of course, it would have been a perfectly good question since there were gods in abundance - gods of love, war, animal fertility, vegetative fertility, of one's country, region, or city. How could anyone understand anything about this Jesus fellow if one did not know which of the many gods had sent him? Monotheism was not unknown in pagan circles, but polytheism was far more widespread. To many pagans, the basic Christian belief in one God meant nothing.

Let us consider another basic Christian presupposition, again derived from the Old Testament. In Acts 2, Luke portrays Peter speaking to the Jews and quoting Joel (2:28-32) and David (Psalm 16:8-11), assuming that citation of Scripture would impress his audience who revered the prophets and considered David to be the author of the psalms. Paul and Barnabas follow the same approach with another Jewish audience (Acts 13:26-41).

But what effect would this approach have had on pagans who did not take the Jewish scriptures as the revealed word of the one God and who were probably puzzled if not actually repulsed at the claim of a conquered people in a frontier province that the God of heaven and earth had made a special pact with them. Probably more than one Christian preacher who cited the Hebrew Scriptures found himself or herself faced with a question like this: "Now, Christian, let me see if I understand you correctly. Your Jesus, a rabble-rouser rightly crucified by our imperial government, was the Son of God because several hundred years earlier some Jewish shepherd said so?" It is not difficult to hear the laughter which would have followed. For many potential or even actual Gentile Christians, the Old Testament was a real problem.

But there is simply no way to make any sense out of Jesus and his message without the Hebrew scriptures. Jesus presumed them and said that he had come to fulfill them.

Antioch, early center for Christian missions

Jewish Christians would have accepted them routinely, and many Gentiles would have done likewise, although less securely, especially after the Jewish War of 66-70 made anything associated with Judaism something to be treated gingerly. As the Gentiles became a majority and then a sizeable majority of the Christians, the temptation to phase away or play down the Old Testament must have been a strong one, but the Christians always remained loyal to the scriptures of their Lord.

The retention of the Old Testament had an important consequence for the composition of the New: it introduced all Christians, Jews and especially Gentiles, to the idea of sacred writings.

There were sacred writings among the pagans, such as the famous Sibylline Books and the writings of Homer, but a priestly college cared for the works of the Sibyl, which could be consulted only by the Roman senate, and the truths of Homer were discovered only through allegory and usually by scholars. There were no pagan equivalents of divinely inspired books intended for the daily life of a whole people and demanding constant study and interpretation. In a strange way, this is an early form of ecumenism: the Jews produced the Old Testament and the Christians gave it to the world.

[In general when the Christians used the Old Testament, they used the Septuagint version, a Greek translation produced initially in Alexandria and used in other areas of the Jewish Dispersion. It was very popular, and in some Jewish circles it was considered as inspired as the Hebrew text. In the second century B.C. an anonymous Jewish author, probably from Alexandria, wrote the so-called *Letter of Aristeas*, which explains the miraculous circumstances under which the initial translation was achieved. The Septuagint, literally "the work of the Seventy," is symbolized by LXX.]

The Gentile mission provided the impetus for the first extant Christian writing, composed about 49. Paul's first missionary journey had resulted in the conversion of many Gentiles, and the question had arisen as to whether these converts should be bound by Jewish regulations, and if so, how many and by how much? At a council in Jerusalem Paul met with the pillars of the Church, Peter, James, and John, and other apostles and elders (Galatians 2:1-10; Acts 15) to discuss this. The council reached the momentous decision that the Gentiles were not bound by these regulations but only by a few "necessary things" (Acts 15:28). The "apostles and elders" (15:22) then communicated their decision to the community at Antioch in what is now the oldest surviving Christian writing, if the letter preserved by Luke in Acts 15:23-29 is authentic. The letter is a considered response to a practical dilemma and based upon ecclesiological principles - even if these were not fully recognized by all the participants (Gal 2:1-10). No one considered the letter to be Scripture in the sense that Old Testament was, but Christian writing had begun.

B. The Pauline Epistles

The next Christian writings are the letters of Paul to the communities which he or his disciples had founded, except for the letter to the Romans and his personal note to Philemon. Exactly which letters are authentically Pauline is uncertain, and I refer the reader to the volumes in the *New Testament Message* series for up-to-date accounts. Here we will just survey the situation.

Most scholars accept Romans, 1-2 Corinthians, Galatians, Philippians, 1 Thessalonians, and Philemon as works of Paul himself. Ephesians is now widely considered post-Pauline. The authenticity of Colossians is much debated, and chances of Pauline authorship are strong. 2 Thessalonians is likewise debated, but a majority of scholars consider it authentic. Almost all scholars now think that the Pastoral Epistles, 1-2 Timothy and Titus are considerably post-Pauline and were written between 100 and 110. Pauline authorship of Hebrews was questioned even in the third century and has been decisively rejected in the twentieth.

Paul was a great theologian and missionary. His theology

is of the highest kind, that is, it seeks to understand the meaning of Jesus Christ not only as a theoretical question but also for the life of the community. All good theologians and pastors have Paul as a model. The theologian who does purely academic theology with no interest in its relation to the church is no different from the activist pastoral person who thinks intellectual activity has no relation to the daily life of the community. Paul's pastoral activity was energetic, extensive, occasionally intimidating, often vivifying, but always attentive to ideas. This mix was good for Paul and good for the Church. To see him only as a theologian is to misunderstand the greater part of his life's work; on the other hand, to see his epistles as occasional writings spurred on by a crisis in one of his communities is to miss the depth of his thought. It is surely no accident some of Paul's most important interpreters, such as Martin Luther and Karl Barth, were both pastors and theologians.

With his epistles, Paul created a new literary form. Study of contemporary letters, preserved mostly in Egyptian papyri, has shown similarities to his epistles, but comparison with those letters has also shown how different Paul was, how he transformed the letter into a vehicle of great power and even of great presence - greater even than his physical presence (cf. 2 Cor. 10:10). The epistle form had a long history in Early Christianity. There are no fewer than twenty-one separate epistles in the New Testament, and seven letters in the Apocalypse (2:1-3:22). Non-canonical, sub-apostolic authors such as Clement of Rome, Ignatius of Antioch, Polycarp of Smyrna, "Barnabas," the anonymous author "To Diognetus," as well as Gnostics such as Ptolemy, all employed this literary form.

Most of Paul's epistles grow from his concern for the community. His earliest letter, 1 Thessalonians, *circa* 50, written in the names of Paul, Silvanus, and Timothy (1:1), exhorts the Thessalonians, left leaderless by his departure (2:17-18), to persevere in faith despite persecution (2:14). Paul fears that his work would come undone and that the Thessalonians might revert to a pagan lifestyle (4:1-8). He also has to allay their fears about the fate of those who died before the Parousia (4:13-18). His second letter to that community, written probably less than a year later, takes up the same themes. He again writes for himself and his co-workers (1:1), urges perseverance in the face of opposition (1:5-12), and again answers questions about the delayed Parousia (2:1-12).

Chronologically the next letter is Galatians, and its communal nature is unquestioned. A serious problem has arisen. Other missionaries have perverted Paul's teaching by insisting that Gentile converts conform to Jewish regulations. Paul sees this as a serious challenge to his mission -which it was - and he reacts angrily, accusing the Galatians of apostasy from the true gospel (1:6-10). He writes only for himself and identifies himself as an apostle called not by men but by Jesus Christ and God the Father (1:1), a point to which we will return in the fourth chapter. The letter itself deals with the relation of the Law to the Gospel, a theological exposition punctuated by pastoral concerns and occasionally by strong personal remarks (3:1 - "O foolish Galatians!").

Paul's next letters, *circa* 55-56, apparently four of them, were to another troubled community, Corinth. Two letters survive, our 1 and 2 Corinthians, although the latter may be a composite piece. 1 Cor 5:9 mentions an earlier letter; some scholars think that a fragment of this is preserved in 2 Cor 6:14-7:1. 2 Cor 2:3-4 refers to a tearful letter, which some scholars think is preserved in 2 Cor 10-13. Neither of these theories has been proved, and the two letters to which Paul refers may be lost for good.

Paul was not the only one writing. 1 Cor 7:1 speaks of a letter the Corinthians wrote to him. In 1:11 of this same epistle Paul speaks of "Chloe's people" who reported to him about the situation in Corinth. [Chloe, apparently some early Christian busybody, is otherwise unknown. In "Chloe to Paul," Benedict Hegarty, O.P., has imaginatively reconstructed her letter; cf. *Sowing the Word*, pp. 225-229.)

Again Paul writes on behalf of fellow workers. 1 Corinthians is from Paul and Sosthenes (1:1), 2 Corinthians from Paul and Timothy (1:1). In each case, however, Paul identifies himself as an apostle, an appellation withheld from the co-workers. If Paul's letters correctly present the situation at Corinth, things were a mess - drunkenness at liturgies, incest, women worshipping without veils (a sign of immodesty in that day), uncontrolled charismatics, and, most seriously, excessive factionalism (1 Cor 1:10-17). Paul wrote firmly and warmly but apparently with limited success. He made a "painful visit" (2 Cor 2:1) to the church there, and yet he had to write again, this time less to solve problems at Corinth than to defend his apostleship and ministry (2 Cor 1:15-3:3; 4:1-6:13; 7:2-16; 11:1-33). As usual, his letters combine brilliant theological and psychological insights (for example, on the nature of love in 1 Cor 13) with direct practical advice.

Paul's most important letter, theologically, is that to the Roman community, which he had not founded nor ever visited. Paul plans to go to Spain (Romans 15:24, 28) and expects to stop in Rome along the way. [Chapter 16 of the epistle is sometimes thought not to be part of the original letter, but here I follow the majority of scholars who think it is indeed part of Romans.] This community was an important one, possibly because of its size and certainly because of its location in the capital of the empire, or, as the Romans would have said it, of the world. We do not know who founded it, and the tradition that Peter was its first bishop is an anachronism, reading back a later practice into the apostolic age. Peter may not have even been in Rome when Paul wrote this epistle, *circa* 58. The community was probably heavily Gentile with a Jewish element. Paul addresses both groups. Much of the letter deals with the Gospel and the Law, a prime concern of Jewish-Christians in Rome who may have heard the accusations of their countrymen that Paul was destroying the Law (Acts 21:27-28), but a legitimate concern also of Gentile converts. If, however, Paul was uncertain of his reception at Rome (the name-dropping in chapter 16 may be a way of ingratiating himself), he does not tone down his views. He discusses the Law frankly with the Romans and apparently won over many of them (Acts 28:14-15).

The last two unquestionably Pauline letters find the apostle in prison, although exactly where is uncertain - probably Rome or Ephesus between 58 and 63. Philippians shows Paul in a surprisingly relaxed mood in spite of his precarious situation (1:21), a sure testimony to his faith in Christ. He talks about his situation to a community he knows and warns the Philippians about false teachers. This epistle is important for including a pre-Pauline Christological hymn (2:6-11).

The letter to Philemon is a gem, a purely personal letter and Paul's only one to an individual. A Christian slave, Onesimus, has run away from his Christian master Philemon. Paul had converted the master and now asks him to take Onesimus back, "no longer as a slave but more than a slave, as a beloved brother" (16).

[This letter has often presented problems for Christians who are surprised that Paul did not ask Philemon to free Onesimus. Paul thought that the world did not have long to last, and people should stay as they are for the duration (1 Cor 7:17-24). He may also have been concerned that the Christian movement, a religious revolution, could be mistaken for a radical social revolution.]

The disputed epistle to the Colossians fits the general pattern of the other epistles. (We follow the assessment of Patrick Rogers in the *NTM* 15 and of Werner Kümmel that Colossians is most likely Pauline.) Paul did not found the church at Colossae, but his co-worker Epaphras did (Col 1:7), so Paul felt justified in writing to the community. Again false teachers were threatening the gospel (2:8-23), and again Paul rose to its defense with a combination of theological insights and pastoral injunctions.

This letter mentions another lost letter of Paul, this one to the nearby community of Laodicea (4:16), making this the fourth (1 Cor 5:9, 7:1, 2 Cor 2:3-4) and possibly the fifth (1 Cor 1:11) such lost letter from this generation of Christians. (Maybe a sixth; cf. 2 Thes 2:2.)

Paul's letters, the earliest New Testament documents, show us a combination of theological and pastoral concerns, a combination which appears in much of the later literature. Supplemented cautiously by Acts, they also show the condition of Christianity down to the early years of the 60s. The next literature will date after the year 70. This is more than a convenient chronological break because between the last of Paul's letters and the writing of the first gospel two events occurred which changed Christianity forever, Nero's persecution of the Christians and the Roman-Jewish War.

C. *The Neronian Persecution*

In the year 64 large parts of the city of Rome burned for several days, causing extensive damage and widespread suffering. The people believed that the emperor Nero (54-68), who by this time had degenerated into a vicious, egomaniacal tyrant, had ordered the fire. Nero tried several different tactics to counteract this belief, but nothing worked, so he decided to shift the blame to someone else. The Roman historian Tacitus says that he chose a group "hated for their abominations, called Christians by the populace." [The "abominations" probably refer to the Christian unwillingness to worship the gods who protected the Empire and also to Christian liturgical terminology ("Eat this body, drink this blood") which led to suspicions of cannibalism.] Nero had the Christians arrested, tortured, and executed. From the 60s until the victorious accession of the emperor Constantine in 312, the danger of persecution existed (there was even one by a pagan emperor in 323), and the Church had to live with that tension.

The persecution also took the lives of Peter and Paul. The New Testament does not mention either death specifically, although John 21:17-19 alludes to Peter's. Christian sources contemporary with or just after the New Testament include the two apostles among the Christian martyrs at Rome.

Nero, persecutor of the Christians.

Previous generations questioned this tradition, but it is widely accepted today.

Historical probability supports it. As we just noted, the Christians had nothing to fear from Rome before this persecution, and Luke shows the Romans acting positively toward Paul (Acts 18:12-16, 19:28-41, 21:30-36, 23:12-35). The Christians in Rome had no reason to hide their identity from the authorities, and the presence in Rome of two prominent members of the sect can hardly have been a secret. When the persecution broke out, Peter and Paul were natural targets for arrest and punishment.

By later standards this first persecution was small and brief, although no less terrible for its victims. But its effects were widespread and echo in the New Testament itself, where the question of Christian attitudes toward the state appears, for example, 1 Peter 2:13-17 or Matthew 22:15-22 (= Mark 12:13-17 and Luke 20:20-26). The concern for the state is understandable. We later generations see Early Christian history in terms of Christianity versus Rome, but most Gentile converts on the contrary would have considered themselves both Roman and Christian. The persecution meant that they now belonged to a group once considered subversive by the government. Even if there were no persecution for another thirty years, the stigma was there, and many Christians would have experienced great qualms of conscience, thus creating a serious pastoral problem for the Church, a problem reflected in the New Testament and partially solved by it (in Acts).

D. The Jewish War

The second event which put an end to the first Christian generation was the great Roman-Jewish war of 66-70, portrayed so vivdly by the Jewish historian Josephus, an eyewitness to much of it. The war was a disaster for the Jews. They fought heroically, and the stand of a resistance group at Masada in 73, three years after the fall of Jerusalem, gained them eternal fame, but it was the Romans who won.

As Luke shows in Acts, the Jerusalem community provided the leadership of the Early Church. But after the destruction of the city, that community fades from importance. The days when the likes of Paul, Barnabas, Peter, and John went to Jerusalem or accepted commissions from that church are gone. The church historian Eusebius says that in the face of Jewish persecution, the community fled east across the Jordan to the town of Pella. It is, however, highly unlikely that the entire community could have fled, and probably some Jewish Christians, reinforced by apocalyptic thinking, chose to fight against the Romans. Here again we must watch out modern notions. Christian non-participation in the war seems sensible to us, but many first-century Jewish Christians, like many Roman Christians, would wish to be loyal to both their faith and their country. In this regard, we should remember that Nero, persecutor of the Christians, was the reigning emperor when the war broke out in 66, and many Jewish-Christians would have had little reason for remaining loyal to the oppressor of their people and the persecutor of their brethren in the faith.

3

THE SECOND GENERATION AND LATER

I. The Gospels

The situation of the second Christian generation, *circa* 70 to 100, differed considerably from that of the first. So did its literature. This generation produced the gospels.

It is impossible to say for sure why the gospels were written. One obvious reason is that those who knew Jesus were dying out, and if the traditions about him were not recorded they would be lost forever. Yet this cannot be the only reason. The earliest gospel, Mark, was composed *circa* 70, or about forty years after Jesus' death. It is difficult to believe that in all that time it never crossed anyone's mind to record what Jesus' disciples had been preaching, especially since some of them had already died, for example, James in 42 (Acts 12:2).

Most scholars today think the gospels were written for much the same reasons as the Pauline epistles, that is, to fulfill the needs of particular communities. Indeed, it is an accepted fact in New Testament studies that the gospels tell us as much about the communities for which they were written as they do of the One about whom they were written.

A. Oral Traditions

Earlier generations considered the gospels to be biographies of Jesus, but today we see them as complex theological documents with equally complex pre-histories, because the gospels were not contemporaneous with Jesus but were written down decades after his death and thus his words and the accounts of his deeds were preserved orally. For generations scholars have tried to understand what factors influenced these oral transmissions which formed the bases for the written gospels and especially how they may have altered the words spoken by Jesus.

Scholars have generally focussed on the theological and eccesiastical factors in the transmission, but before we look at those, we should note that some factors were purely "human," that is, they were unintentional and unconscious. For example, a disciple who was asked to tell a community what Jesus had to say might simply have forgotten exactly what Jesus said, and so he or she simply approximated the words. In other cases, the disciple involved thought a paraphrase would do. For example, if Bob met Amy and said to her, "If you see Alicia, please tell her I said 'Hello,'" and Amy, when she meets Alicia, says, "Bob says, 'Hi,' " most of us would agree that Amy had faithfully passed along Bob's message, but, of course, she did not pass along his exact words. A Christian disciple who knew Jesus' words to be "by the Father" but said "by my Father" might simply have thought that it did not really make a difference and thus did not bother to correct it. Finally, there is the very obvious problem of words spoken by Jesus in his native language of Aramaic but which Christian missionaries had to render into Greek or Latin or Syriac. As anyone who has ever studied foreign languages on any level knows, some phrases are virtually impossible to translate exactly, and this no doubt happened to words of Jesus.

The theological and ecclesiastical factors center on the preservation work of teachers and proclaimers, who did what teachers and proclaimers still do - they adapted the material for their audiences. This means that the material about Jesus which had the most relevance to the first communities stood the best chance of being preserved; conversely, that which had the least relevance ran the greatest risk of being lost. In short, there was a process of selectivity in the preservation of Jesus' words and deeds. (To test this, get hold of an older Bible, one which has Jesus' words printed in red to distinguish them from the evangelist's narrative, and read the words out loud. It should take you about half an hour per gospel - half an hour's worth of words from Jesus' entire public career!)

There was another important consequence to the preservation of Jesus' words by teachers and proclaimers. Individual sayings might be particularly apt in a given situation, and the teacher/proclaimer used it apart from its initial setting in Jesus' life. The inevitable happened. In the course of time the saying floated free from the setting. For example, consider the saying "Foxes have holes and birds of the air have nests, but the Son of Man has nowhere to lay his head." In Matthew's gospel Jesus says this to one of the scribes just before he gets into a boat with his disciples for the trip that required his miraculous stilling of the storm (Matthew 8:18-27). In Luke's gospel Jesus utters this saying to an unidentified man while he is walking along a road with his disciples (Luke 9:57-58); furthermore the stilling of the storm occurs not after the saying but some time before it (Luke 8:22-25). The saying had clearly become separated from its original context and then reset in at least one and possibly both of these gospels.

But the sayings and deeds of Jesus were not, so to speak, dropped in a tin can and then pulled out from time to time as the occasion warranted. It appears that the Passion narrative was always something of a continuous whole, and it is likely that other events in Jesus' life were retold in a general chronological sequence. After a time - and no one can be sure exactly when - strands of material were organized into what scholars call *Q* from the German word *Quelle*, "source." *Q* was apparently a collection of material about Jesus which was preserved as a body in more than one church since elements of it appear in the gospels of Matthew and Luke. Individual sayings from Q can be isolated, but Q's exact nature and extent are uncertain.

The Q material could have been both written and oral. We find it difficult to imagine memorizing large amounts of material, but we are literate and do not have to rely heavily upon our memories. Many ancient peoples were non-literate and could rely only on their memories. A shrewd ancient obsever, Julius Caesar, marvelled at how much the non-literate druids of Gaul could memorize, and he pointed out that the Romans, who could write, had let their memories atrophy. Yet even literate people in the ancient world had memories which would surprise us. As late as the fifth century, as St. Augustine tells us in his *Confessions*, extensive memorization of Latin verse was a standard part of the school curriculum. Notice how easily Jesus and the people he spoke with are able to cite the Scriptures and Jewish law from memory.

Thus, the words of Jesus were passed along orally and no doubt they were affected by this passing along or tradition, from the Latin *traditio*, "a handing over," including the handing over of something from one generation to another. This material was shaped by the various local communities, who treated it with a freedom unimaginable to later generations. For example, if a certain saying were given a certain nuance, the nuance could become added to the saying and passed along with it as a new whole. Compare Luke 6:20-21 with Matthew 5:3 and 5:6; "Blessed are you poor" versus "Blessed are the poor in spirit," and "Blessed are you that hunger now" versus "Blessed are those who hunger and thirst for righteousness." The sayings from Luke show Jesus directly addressing social outcasts who suffer specific physical privations (money and food), while those from Matthew moderate Jesus into a general ethical teacher whose third-person words can apply to all classes since even the rich can be poor in spirit and even those who are well fed can hunger and thirst for righteousness. Somewhere behind both sets of sayings are Jesus' original words.

This freedom may surprise us, but we know from the books of the Old Testament prophets that disciples could speak in the name of their masters, even if those masters had been dead for generations, for example, Second Isaiah and Third Isaiah, as well as the pseudonymous (falsely-named) works of the Old and New Testaments.

Many fundamentalist Christians who spurn modern exegesis may object that this process means that we do not have access to Jesus himself but only to the Early Church's Jesus. That objection is true but it is also meaningless. Remember that Jesus wrote nothing himself, so if we reject what the Early Church tells us about him, we would know nothing about him at all, except for meager and usually hostile references in non-Christian sources. This is not the opinion of 'modern' exegesis; it is a simple fact. We simply cannot separate the words of Jesus from the communities which preserved them; we cannot separate Jesus from his church; and we have no right to assume he would have made such a separation.

B. Mark

About the year 70 Mark decided to write his *evangelion*, his "good news" or gospel. Who was "Mark"? An early second-century bishop named Papias first identified the author of the second gospel as one Mark who was an interpreter (*hermeneut*) of Peter. Another early Christian writer, Clement of Alexandria (*ca.* 200), said that Mark wrote his gospel at the request of the Roman community but while Peter was still alive. Modern scholarship, especially Anglo-American, has largely accepted the identification of this Mark with the (John) Mark who appears in isolated places in the New Testament (Acts 12:12-17, 13:5-13, 15:36-39; Col 4:10; Phm 24; 2 Tim 4:11; 2 Peter 5:13). There are basically two reasons for this. First, the tradition does not conflict with the internal evidence of the gospel, for example, Mark's uses several Latin words, so there is no *a priori* reason to reject it. Second, if the writer were not Mark, why would someone put that name on the gospel? Why not use one of the unclaimed members of the Twelve, such as

Andrew or Philip, to give the gospel more authority? As we shall see in chapter four, many Gnostic writers used that approach and with considerable success. The name of the gospel is most easily understood as a witness to its author. If, however, Mark did write the gospel at the urging of the Roman community, he wrote the completed version after Peter's death in the persecution when the need to preserve Peter's words was glaringly apparent. It is significant that the oldest traditions about the oldest gospel attribute its origin to community demands.

[This does not, however, mean that the identification of John Mark with the evangelist is certain; some modern scholars would locate the gospel's origin in Syria.]

All the gospels are complex theological documents with themes and sub-themes, and there are many good commentaries which explain all this. Here I would like to adhere to our main theme, the New Testament in the life of the Church, and to see how Mark addressed the needs of the community. Mark's main interest is naturally the person of Jesus, but his presentation of Jesus must have surprised many Christians outside Mark's community. Paul shows us that Christian hymns exalted Jesus (Phil 2:9), and Paul himself speaks of the Lord of glory (1 Cor 2:8), even though Jesus had been crucified. But Mark's Jesus enjoys little glory. He cannot fulfill his mission and still be great in the eyes of the world; indeed, he must actively discourage those who think that way (Mark's famous "Messianic Secret"). He can win glory only by humiliation and suffering and rejection and death. When Jesus tries to explain this to his disciples ("he said this plainly" - 8:32), no less than Peter tries to dissuade him from his plan, only to be rebuked as Satan (8:33). The young man at the tomb gives a one-verse witness to Jesus' ultimate triumph (16:6), but otherwise the gospel tries to prepare the reader not for glory but for suffering. If the Roman location for the gospel is accurate, then this well suited the needs of the post-persecution Roman community. The sufferings and deaths of relatives and friends and the loss of two great Christian leaders, as well as the possibility that with the precedent set, another persecution could occur, must have devastated and demoralized the Roman Christians. Mark met their needs admirably. He offered neither polyanna-like hopes nor apocalyptic deprecations against the persecutors. Instead he reminded the Christians that they were followers of Jesus Christ, who himself had suffered unjustly but who was glorified through his sufferings. If he had to suffer, could his followers expect less? If he endured it, could his followers do less? Mark's message was not an easy one - it still is not - but it was a thoroughly Christian one.

Mark's gospel inaugurated a new era by preserving in writing some of Jesus' words and deeds. It was truly an epoch-making document, destined to be imitated by many authors well into the second century and beyond. The "gospel" became *the* vehicle for knowing Jesus.

C. Oral Tradition after Mark

Before seeing how others followed Mark, we must pause to remember that the beginning of one era does not necessarily mean the end of an earlier one. Just because Jesus' words had been written down does not mean that oral tradition ceased immediately. With our infallible hindsight we know that the future lay with written records, but that was hardly obvious to Christians *circa* 70. Most of them still knew of Jesus via oral preaching and teaching, and its popularity was not just a question of numbers. On the contrary, oral tradition had worked well for about a forty-year period which had seen the Church survive persecutions by Jews and pagans, formulate a rudimentary Christology, and spread from Jerusalem to much of the Mediterranean world. There was simply no good reason to discard oral tradition, and most Christians did not. In fact, the second-century bishop Papias, who first told us Mark wrote a gospel, says that he *preferred* oral traditions to written ones. It is quite common in reading second-century Christian writers to come across phrases which approximate passages in the gospels, and while in some cases it is likely the author has tried unsuccessfully to cite a gospel from memory, in other cases he almost certainly is relying on an oral tradition. There are also several sayings attributed to Jesus by later writers which are not preserved in the gospels. They may not be authentic, but they prove the persistence of oral traditions. How long the oral traditions maintained themselves against the gospels is uncertain; no doubt the situation varied from community to community. For example, a church without its own gospel but founded by Paul or Barnabas or Epaphroditus might be more apt to cling to oral traditions going back to the founder than to adopt a newer and, perhaps, therefore "lesser" authority.

But the written gospel was to prevail. Mark's gospel was well-known and heavily used by two other evangelists, Luke and Matthew. Chronologically the two are contemporary (*circa* 80-90), and no one can be certain if one of these depended upon the other. We will consider Luke first.

D. Luke

"Luke" has been identified from the second century with the Luke who appears in several epistles (Col 4:14; Phm 24; 2 Tim 4:11) and with the companion of Paul in the "we" sections of Acts (16:10-17, 20:5-21:18, 27:1-28:16) since there is no question that the same person wrote Luke and Acts. As is the case with Mark, the certain proof is lacking, but there is no compelling reason to reject the identification. There is also the question of why someone would pick an obscure figure like Luke when so many prominent names in Paul's circle, such as Timothy and Titus were available. We will accept Luke as the author of the third gospel.

There is no firm tradition about where Luke wrote the gospel, although the oldest account says Greece, which does not conflict with the internal evidence. He is the New Testament writer most likely to have been a Gentile; he fully supported Paul's universalism.

Luke dedicates the gospel to someone named Theophilus (1:1), and he speaks of "many (who) have undertaken to compile a narrative of the things which have just been accomplished among us," that is, the career of Jesus. Luke used Mark's gospel, and there is the possibility that he knew Matthew's, but even if he did, two hardly constitutes "many." Perhaps Luke had in mind a written form of *Q*. We do not know who the "many" were nor what they wrote, but apparently some accounts of Jesus' career were available for Luke to consult.

Luke reflects the post-70 Christian world. For him Paul's conflicts with the Law are a thing of the past; they are of historical interest but no more. Luke wrote for an obviously Gentile church, and some scholars detect anti-Semitism in his gospel, possibly a reaction to the taint of sedition which the Jewish revolt gave to what had been a largely Jewish religion.

Luke's community interests are boldly obvious. Many Jews considered themselves the Chosen People, an ethnic identification. Paul and other Christians who thought as he did had made it clear that although Christ had come first to the Jews, his message was for all nations. Luke infuses this message into page after page of his gospel, but his universalism is also social, reaching to all classes, including outcasts, such as poor people and criminals. Luke's Jesus traces his descent back to Adam, the father of all nations (3:23-38). Simeon announces that the baby boy is a light of revelation to the nations (2:32). Only Luke tells the stories of the widow's son, the Good Samaritan, the prodigal son, Lazarus the blessed poor man, the Pharisee and the publican, and the good thief on the cross. There can be no doubt: salvation is for everyone.

The universalism appears in many subtler ways. Matthew (17:15) and Mark (9:17) speak of an epileptic boy whom Jesus heals simply as a man's son. Luke (9:38) adds that he was the man's *only* son in order to heighten the pathos and thus magnify the concern of Jesus for the unfortunate. All three synoptic gospels tell of Jesus' rejection at Nazareth (Matt 13:54-58, Mark 6:1-6, Luke 4:16-30), but in Luke alone does Jesus tell the Nazarenes that Elijah ministered only to Gentiles. Matthew speaks of many who will "come from east and west and sit at table with Abraham, Isaac, and Jacob in the kingdom of heaven" while the lost are excluded and weep and gnash their teeth (Matt 8:11-12). Luke changes this just enough to universalize it (13:28-29): "There you will weep and gnash your teeth, when you see Abraham and Isaac and Jacob and all the prophets in the kingdom of God and you yourselves thrust out. And men will come from east and west, and from north and south, and sit at table in the kingdom of God." For Luke the men come from all four directions, a symbol of the whole world. More subtly, the three great Jewish patriarchs are joined with "all the prophets," and since there were Christian prophets (Acts 11:27, 13:1, 21:9) the historical uniqueness of the patriarchs is weakened. In Matthew's gospel the saved receive their reward by sitting with the patriarchs; Luke mentions only the table in the kingdom of God.

As a Christian, Luke could not and would not deny his Jewish heritage, for example, Luke 1-2, but as a writer to a Gentile community, he has toned it down. To his credit, however, he has done it the right way. He does not denounce Judaism but emphasizes the positive achievement of Jesus in coming to save everyone. This message must have been a welcome one in Gentile communities.

E. Matthew

Matthew's gospel was written *circa* 80-90, and most scholars would locate it in Syria, probably in Antioch or its environs. Christian tradition from the second century identifies "Matthew" with the tax collector of Matt 9:9 who became one of the Twelve. But modern scholarship unanimously rejects this for a number of reasons, the most compelling being Matthew's obvious reliance upon Mark's gospel. Why would a member of the Twelve - and therefore an eyewitness to much of what he wrote about - borrow material from someone whose account was at best second hand? "Matthew" is anonymous, and there is no way of knowing how and why the name Matthew became attached to the gospel, except that the author wanted to give it the authority of one of the Twelve.

Another second-century tradition scholars reject is of an "Aramaic Matthew," that is, the theory based upon a statement of bishop Papias that Matthew originally "composed his discourses in the Hebrew tongue," that is, in Aramaic, and thus that our Matthew is a translation of this now-lost work or at least that an Aramaic original underlies the extant gospel. Literary analysis demonstrates that the extant gospel was originally written in fluent Greek and so is not a translation. In addition, it is a well-drafted narrative and shows no traces of being a revision of another work. Possibly some sort of Jesus -narrative in Aramaic circulated in the first and second centuries, but the only evidence for it is Papias. Finally, the possibility that such a work once existed has no bearing on the understanding of the extant gospel.

In the recent book *Antioch and Rome*, John Meier says that "Matthew's gospel must be seen as a theological and pastoral response to a crisis of self-identity and function in the Antiochene church, . . . (p. 52)" Among the people for whom the evangelist shows great concern are Jewish-Christians who were set adrift by the disaster of the Jewish War and the decline of the Jerusalem community's influence. They felt torn between their people and their old religion on the one hand and their new, increasingly Gentile-dominated faith on the other. They believed that God had spoken to Israel, and that the Jewish people as a people had a role to play in Christianity. They must have been concerned about Christians like Luke who thought little of the law, and they must have wondered about the wisdom of Paul's course since even Christians he himself had evangelized thought that Christianity brought freedom from all laws and that sexual license was permitted (1 Cor 6:12-20). These Jewish Christians experienced an acute psychological dilemma, and Matthew tried to alleviate it.

Like Mark he took an admirable course. He made it very clear that there are good Gentiles and they belong in Christianity (8:5-13, 15:21-28, 20:1-16, 28:19-20). He also makes it clear that Jesus' own people rejected him (14:53-58, 27:25). Matthew occasionally linked these two themes of Jewish rejection and Gentile acceptance (2:1-18, 21:33-44, 22:1-14). These realities were not easy pills for his Jewish readers to swallow, but Matthew is honest with them. The message is for every people whether the Jewish-Christians like it or not. It was inevitable that some of the Gentiles would prove unworthy (22:11-14), but they still have a place in the Church. The Jews should consider, however painfully, their responsibility in creating this tension. To ignore or gloss over these realities is to achieve nothing.

On the other hand, throughout his gospel Matthew reassures his Jewish-Christian readers about the nature of Christianity. His is the gospel containing Jesus' words, "think not that I have come to abolish the Law and the prophets; I have not come to abolish them but to fulfill them" (5:17). And for those who might think that this fulfillment has occurred and that the moral precepts of the Jews have become things of the past, Matthew adds three verses later, "For I tell you unless your righteousness exceeds that of the scribes and the Pharisees (known for their strict adherence to legal regulations), you will never enter the kingdom of heaven." In Matthew's eyes, faith in Jesus does not reject or discard the old religion but rather brings it to new heights. This technique is both clever and effective. Matthew has reassured his readers but also made them feel special again. Unlike the Gentiles, they know what went before; unlike the Gentiles, they understand just what Jesus has done.

Matthew's concern for his Jewish-Christian readers appears immediately in the gospel. He opens with Jesus' genealogy which he traces to Abraham, father of the Jewish people, through David, the greatest of Jewish kings (1:1-17). [Contrast this with Luke who traces the genealogy back to Adam, father of all races (Luke 3:23-38).] The infancy narrative follows next, and although it shows believing Gentiles (the Magi) and unbelieving Jews (Herod and his court), these events occur to fulfill no fewer than five prophecies (1:23, 2:6, 2:15, 2:18, 2:23), something Jewish readers would appreciate. They would also appreciate Matthew's comparison of the infancies of Jesus and Moses (Exodus 1-2). An evil king, fearful for his throne, orders the execution of male infants, but the sacred hero escapes, leaves the country, and returns later. This Jesus-Moses comparison appears later in chapters 5-7 where Jesus gives the Sermon on the Mount, echoing Moses' reception of the Law on Mount Sinai (Exo 19-20).

Like the other evangelists, Matthew can be quietly effective. We saw earlier how he and Luke described the table in the kingdom. Here we see how he treated an issue of special concern to Jewish converts, the Christian attitude toward the Law.

Mark tells this story (2:23-28).

> One sabbath he was going through the grainfields; and as they made their way his disciples began to pluck ears of grain. And the Pharisees said to him, "Look, why are they doing what is not lawful on the sabbath?" And he said to them, "Have you never read what David did when he was in need and was hungry, he and those with him; how he entered the house of God, when Abiathar was high priest, and ate the bread of the Presence, which it is not lawful for any but the priests to eat, and also gave it to those who were with him?" And he said to them, "The sabbath was made for man, not man for the sabbath; so the Son of man is lord even of the Sabbath."

In this account Jesus makes a mistake. 1 Samuel 21:1-6 says that Ahimelech, not Abiathar, was the priest when David ate the bread. This would not bother us because we know that Jesus was like to us in all things except sin (Hebrews 4:15), so he was certainly human enough for a slip of the memory. But it did bother Luke who in his version of the story (6:1-11) simply dropped the reference to Abiathar. (He might have wanted to correct it to Ahimelech, but Mark's gospel was known, so a discreet omission was better.) Luke also added some details, and he omitted others, but he basically reproduced Mark.

Yet look how differently Matthew tells the story (12:1-8).

> At that time Jesus went through the grainfields on the sabbath; his disciples were hungry and began to pluck ears of grain and to eat. But when the Pharisees saw it, they said to him, "Look, your disciples are doing what is not lawful to do on the sabbath." He said to them, "Have you not read what David did, when he was hungry and those who were with him: how he entered the house of God and ate the bread of the Presence, which it was not lawful for him to eat nor for those who were with him, but only for the priests? Or have you not read in the law how on the sabbath the priests in the temple profane the sabbath and are guiltless? I tell you, something greater than the temple is here. And if you had known what this means, 'I desire mercy and not sacrifice,' you would not have condemned the guiltless. For the Son of man is lord of the sabbath."

It concerns Matthew that Jesus and his disciples appear to take a cavalier attitude toward the Sabbath. As Lord of the Sabbath, Jesus requires no excuse; as ordinary Jews, the disciples do, so Matthew says they were hungry. This may not excuse them in everyone's eyes, but at least it provides a reason for their behavior. Matthew next moderates the attitude of the Pharisees who point out to Jesus what his disciples are doing, thus giving Jesus the benefit of the doubt since he is possibly unaware of what they are doing. In Mark the Pharisees directly ask Jesus why his disciples are plucking grain, thus saying that he knew not only what they were doing but also why. Luke's Pharisees are even more direct and accuse Jesus himself: "Why are you doing what is not lawful to do on the Sabbath?" (6:2).

Matthew's Pharisees are fair to Jesus, and he replies honorably to them. He cites the same passage as Mark and Luke, although again without Abiathar, not only because like Luke Matthew did not want to portray Jesus making a mistake, but also because he did not want to show Jesus ignorant of Jewish history. Then Matthew goes on to cite a second example found "in the law" (12:5), thus making a stronger case for his position, which in turn is a tacit acknowledgment of respect for the Pharisees and their position. This also presents to Matthew's readers a Jesus who relies upon Jewish precedents. Matthew closes his account by affirming that Pharisees in this case spoke against Jesus from ignorance. Jesus is made to say that had they known differently, they would have acted differently. He leaves out Mark's remark about the sabbath being made for man, possibly not wanting to compromise its divinely ordained authority.

We do not know if this gospel met the reservations of its Jewish-Christian readers, but we can see once more that the scriptural author, although independent and original, wrote for communal needs.

F. John

Scholars have long known that John's gospel emerged from a unique community because its general concerns and its portrayal of Jesus differ so much from the synoptic gospels. Raymond Brown, in his *The Community of the Beloved Disciple*, made a study of this community, and much of what follows draws from that book.

Since the second century Christian tradition has named John the apostle, one of the Twelve, as the author of the fourth gospel. No modern scholars hold that view, although some will concede that the witness of John son of Zebedee stands behind the gospel. But the unavoidable Papias speaks of a John the Elder or John the Presbyter who wrote 2 and 3 John. There is also the John who wrote the Apocalypse, whom no one now considers to be the apostle or the author of the gospel. Since the traditional location of the Johannine community is Western Asia Minor, Ephesus specifically, and since the seven letters in the Apocalypse are written to Western Asian churches, there is a real possibility that two or three Christians named John resided in that area when the gospel was written. (The name is common. Even a limited range of books like those of the New Testament includes John the Baptist, John the son of Zebedee, John Mark, and John the apocalyptist.)

Brown sees the Johannine commnity as one which consciously separated itself from the pagans, Jews, and other Christian groups, although it did not actually break from the last. The community grouped itself around an obscure figure called the Beloved Disciple (John 13:23, 19:26, 20:2-9, 21:20-24) whom tradition has identified as John son of Zebedee. The reference in 21:20-24 makes it clear that this man stands behind the gospel, even though it was redacted by someone else since 21:23 implies that the Beloved Disciple has died and this should not be a cause for shock or concern by anyone.

After the disciple's death the community suffered a serious schism, and Brown thinks the smaller part, represented in the New Testament by the three Johannine epistles, joined the larger Church, while the rest drifted off into gnosticism or Montanism, which we will consider in later chapters.

While we cannot be sure exactly what moved the original community to separation from the larger Church, its high Christology may have been a factor. This community emphasized the heavenly Jesus, the pre-existing being who came down from heaven to take the form of a man. The gospel never denies Jesus' humanity, but its author was not very comfortable with the form that humanity took.

The well-known prologue (1:1-18), which used to close the Latin mass (although only to verse 14), makes the case for the pre-existing Christ, but the just-more-than-human Jesus is introduced quietly into a variety of places. The crucifixion, an embarrassing, lowly death, is spoken of as a lifting up (3:14, 8:28, 12:32). Jesus mysteriously knows the background of a woman he had never met before (4:16-18). He asks the disciples a question, but John assures us that Jesus already knew the answer (6:5-6). He knows who among the disciples will betray him (6:64). He knows that he will be arrested (18:4), and it is something he is willing to accept (18:11) although he literally floors his captor with the sound of his voice (18:6). Jesus assures Pilate that if his kingship were of this world, his followers would have prevented his arrest (18:36). In sum, John has carefully avoided giving Jesus any human weaknesses, especially ignorance.

This more-than-human dimension is reflected in the constant use of darkness and light, for example, the prologue (1:1-18), the curing of the blind man (ch. 9), "the light of the world" discourse (8:12-59), and the clever use of surface questions to reveal deeper meanings as Jesus brings the people to light (3:1-21, 4:1-42). The prologue has established the cosmic theme (1:5), and the man Jesus fights the cosmic battle.

John's gospel includes another dimension which strongly proves his communal concerns. Christians share many things, but the only thing they do as a community is to worship. John's gospel is replete with liturgical images. To the Samaritan woman Jesus speaks of the water of life (4:7-15). The pool of Bethsaida has water which restores health (5:1-18). After the miracle of the multiplication of loaves to feed the five thousand, Jesus talks of the bread of God come down from heaven and identifies himself as the bread of life (6:22-71). A liturgical setting also explains one of the most curious passages in the gospel, 19:34: "But one of the soldiers pierced his side with a spear, and at once there came out blood and water." This is a possible but very unlikely biological phenomenon, and scholars interpret it as being a Johannine sign rather than an historical event, that is, the blood (eucharist) and water (baptism) flow from the body of Christ (the Church). John's is not the only gospel to include liturgical references, but it is the only one to make liturgy a central theme.

Eventually this unique view of Jesus would be accepted by the Church at large, and it would play a great role in Christology. This small community, striving for self-definition, opened a new, creative perspective for all Christians.

Four evangelists, four communities, four accounts of Jesus and his work. Far from proving the unreliability or even falsity of the various accounts, they prove the vitality and involvement of the first Christians in making their savior a living reality in their midst.

II. The Later Books of the New Testament

The gospels and Pauline epistles are the most important and widely studied books of the New Testament, but they make up not quite half of its number (13 of 27). Of the remaining fourteen books, twelve are epistles, and all of them have a clearly pastoral character, that is, they respond to community needs.

A. The Pastorals

The most obviously pastoral are, of course, the Pastoral Epistles (1-2 Timothy, Titus). For generations they were thought to be Pauline because the author calls himself Paul and gives some specific directions to the Pauline disciples who are the supposed recipients of the letters. But the literary style and the organized church life presumed in the epistles make Pauline authorship impossible. Scholars date the epistles anywhere from 80 to 150, but the tendency is toward 100-110. The locations of the author and recipients are uncertain, although the latter were probably in communities founded by Paul or one of his disciples, which would put them most likely in Asia Minor.

Living in a more settled ecclesial situation than Paul, the pseudonymous author is very concerned about church offices and discipline. He also confronts another problem of a settled community, false teaching. Many converts have been made and they have brought with them new traditions and new questions, and some of them were reaching new conclusions. "Such are Hymenaeus and Philetus; they have shot wide of the truth in saying that the resurrection has already taken place, and they are upsetting people's faith" (2 Timothy 2:17-18). The author of the Pastorals sees the danger in this, and he tries to combat it. Probably lacking the moral authority to act decisively, he writes under the name of Paul, whose authority he expects the endangered communities to respect. He follows Paul in aligning right belief with right living, and he continuously intersperses his warnings about false teachers (1 Tim 1:3-20, 2 Tim 2:14-4:8, Titus 1:10-16) with teachings or exhortations about Christian living (1 Tim 2:1-3:16, 2 Tim 1:3-2:13, Titus 2:1-15). It is, however, clear that he lacks Paul's overweening confidence in himself, his faith, and the spirit, or, to put it more briefly, his apostolic calling. That is probably why he talks about the qualities of church ministers and the obligations of church members. Structure is independent of personalities.

B. The Johannine Epistles

In *The Community of the Beloved Disciple*. Brown argues strongly for the pastoral setting of the Johannine epistles, composed shortly after the gospel, *circa* 100-110, and for the same community. The author of the first epistle may be the redactor of the gospel; he is concerned to apply some of its principles in more concrete situations. But the anonymous author faces a more pressing problem: schism within his own community. A group has left, and the author is trying to put the best face on this by saying that the schismatics were never really members of the group (2:19). Yet the dissidents apparently had some success in winning new converts (4:5). The author justifies his situation by claiming divine support, for example, 4:6: "We are of God. Whoever knows God listens to us and he who does not know God does not listen to us." It is unlikely he hoped to win back the schismatics but rather wished to shore up the spirit of his group and to ward off any more defections.

2-3 John are possibly by the same author as 1 John; certainly they emerge from the same general community. The author is again anonymous, but he identifies himself as "the elder" or "the presbyter." Since presbyters were not uncommon in the Early Church (Acts 11:30, 15:2, 20:17; 1

Tim 4:14; James 5:14, 1 Peter 5:1), the title in this instance may be more honorary than institutional.

In 2 John he writes to "the elect lady and her children," probably a personification of the local church. He warns this ecclesial family about false teachers - possibly the schismatics - and urges them to love one another and follow right doctrine.

In 3 John the elder writes to a Christian brother Gaius who apparently heads a local community. The elder praises his well-known hospitality to strangers (v. 6), that is, Christians from other churches, but he is shocked at the behavior of Diotrephes, who enjoys heading another community and whose arrogance extends to criticizing the elder, rejecting his authority, refusing hospitality to visitors associated with him, and expelling from his (Diotrephes') community those who protest this wanton violation of the obligation of Christian hospitality. The elder, however, appears powerless to do anything about this. He finishes his letter by commending Demetrius, probably the letter carrier, to Gaius, and he expresses hope for a personal visit. Gaius, Diotrephes, and Demetrius are known to us only from this epistle, a rare gem which gives us a glimpse of how the Early Christians adjusted to everyday ecclesial life.

C. Peter, James, and Jude

The remaining four Catholic epistles likewise fit easily into a pastoral category. 1 Peter dates *circa* 80-90 and is by a member of the Christian community in Rome, or, as the author calls it, "Babylon" (5:13), an image which reappears in the Apocalypse (chs. 17-18). He writes (1:1) "to those of God's scattered people who lodge for a while in Pontus, Galatia, Cappadocia, Asia, and Bithynia," that is, in Asia Minor. ("Asia" means the Roman province of Asia on the western end of the peninsula.) Obviously this letter was intended for more than one church, a practice we encountered before (Col 4:16) although not as extensively.

The Christians were experiencing some kind of persecution (4:12-16), but we cannot be sure what it was, that is, formal persecution by the government or just the hostility of resentment and prejudice. There is some evidence for persecution in Asia Minor *circa* 90, but nothing extensive enough to cover the whole peninsula, so it was probably social rather than official persecution which concerns "Peter." Formal persecution is more dangerous in the short run because it takes lives or property, yet conversely it also brings people together in a sense of shared oppression and opposition, and it sharply defines a group. But quiet, unspectacular coolness can have a more debilitating effect in the long run. "Why are we different?" "Those other people don't seem too bad; why don't they like us?" "Maybe if we just change this little thing, we'd get along better with them." Sentiments like this were probably heard in more than one Christian community.

The author used Peter's authority in what can only be called an exhortation. He urges the faithful to maintain a holy life (1:13-2:10), to keep Christian standards in a world challenging or rejecting those standards (2:11-3:12), and to endure outside pressures (3:13-4:6). He still believed in an imminent Parousia, and he urges his readers to prepare for it (4:12-19). He closed with some instructions for his fellow presbyters (5:1-11). He obviously hoped to keep his readers strong for just a while longer until Jesus came again. Little could he know for how long they would have to be strong or how long his words would be with them.

The epistle of James is not by the brother of the Lord, leader of the Jerusalem community; possibly the writer was a disciple of his. Scholars date the epistle *circa* 90-100, considerably later than James' martyrdom in 62. The author is a Jewish-Christian writing for other Jewish-Christians, whom he identifies as "the Twelve Tribes in the Dispersion" (1:1). Like 1 Peter, this is a general letter. The places of origin and destination are unknown. The pastoral nature is so strong that many scholars think it is a homily in letter form. It deals with Christian ethical behavior, sometimes with generalities (1:19-21, 4:1-10), occasionally with specifics (2:1-7).

The epistle of James endured much criticism from Martin Luther and others who abhorred its emphasis on the need for good works rather than on salvation by faith and grace. But "James," like other Jewish-Christians, may have been concerned about distortions of Paul's teachings. Paul knew what he meant by salvation by faith, but, as every teacher and lecturer knows, what you say and how your hearers understand it are two different things. Some Christians probably thought that if they had faith (defined by them as right belief), they could do what they liked. But James points out that even the demons believe in one God (2:19), and no one was likely to consider them Christians.

In 2:18-26, James discusses Abraham's righteousness by faith (Genesis 15:6). Depending on one's view, his treatment is either a complement or an antidote to Paul's discussion in Romans 4:1-12, because there is no doubt that James has that Pauline passage in mind. In Christian history, Paul's words have always carried more weight than James', but the latter has always provided a good counterbalance to extreme interpretations of Paul, because surely "faith apart from good works is dead" (2:26).

The very brief epistle of Jude is also pseudonymous. Most scholars date it as late as 100, too late to be written by one of the Twelve, and the Greek style is too good for a Palestinian Jew of probably modest circumstances. The place of composition is unknown, and the audience is uncertain since it is addressed "to those who are called, beloved in God the Father and kept for Jesus Christ" (v. 1). Jude responded to an emergency situation; false teachers had surreptitiously infiltrated the community and were attempting to corrupt it. Jude empahsizes the damnation these teachers would meet (5-16) and tells the people how to respond to their teaching. This is not very encouraging reading, but it is decidedly pastoral.

2 Peter is also pseudonymous, and scholars date it *circa* 125. The letter refers to 1 Peter (2 Peter 3:1) so it was probably sent to one or more of the communities which received the earlier letter, that is, somewhere in Asia Minor,

and it is probably written from a Petrine center. In 125 this would most likely have been Rome.

The letter has importance for the history of the canon, and we will discuss it in the next chapter. Here we just note that "Peter," like the authors of the Pastorals and the other Catholic Epistles, has to deal with the threat of false teachers, whom he strongly condemns. His last chapter deals with the delay of the Parousia, which may have been an opening for the false teachers ("They said Jesus would come back, but he hasn't. Why should we listen to them on other matters?").

D. Ephesians

Any discussion of the epistle to the Ephesians revolves around the question of Pauline authorship, asserted in the epistle's opening words (1:1). The issue is very complex, and in *The Jerome Biblical Commentary* Joseph Grassi says the question of authenticity is currently insoluble (II, 342). Most scholars consider the work post-Pauline, and many of them think this hortatory epistle was composed as an introduction to the authentic Pauline letters. Yet there are still many who think Paul wrote the epistle, either himself or through a secretary, and in three recent English-language commentaries the *Anchor Bible* (vol. 34), the *Cambridge Bible Commentary*, and *New Testament Message* (vol. 14), Pauline authorship is defended. The authorship issue affects theories on the time of composition, for example, the early 60s if Paul wrote it, *circa* 80-100 if not Paul; and the place of writing, for example, Rome if by Paul since he three times mentions being in prison (3:1, 4:1, 6:20) and an undetermined location if not Paul. We humbly side with those who consider the question currently insoluble.

The authenticity question does not affect our basic thesis, that this epistle, like most of the other epistles, has a pastoral character. In fact, so pastoral is its character that parties on both sides of the authorship debate suggest that Ephesians may actually be not an epistle but a homily since it falls well into two parts, a doctrinal one (1:3-3:21) and a moralizing one (4:1-6:20), and the doctrinal part even has sections which sound like prayers (1:3-10, 3:14-20).

E. Hebrews

Our last epistle is that to the Hebrews. Although generations of Christians considered it Pauline, its authenticity has always been questioned, largely because its style diverges considerably from that of unquestioned Pauline works. The third-century Alexandrian scholar Origen (*ca.* 185-254) suggested that Luke or Paul's fellow-worker Clement (Phil 4:3) might have written it, but Origen concluded that "the true author is known to God alone" (Eusebius, *H.E.* 6.26). Modern scholars agree completely.

Hebrews was intended for a Jewish-Christian audience because its main theme (nine and a half chapters of thirteen) is with Jesus Christ as the new, true, and eternal high priest whose priesthood supersedes that of the Old Testament. The argument is sophisticated and presumes some developed theological notions on the part of the audience. Scholars date this some time after Paul (*circa* 80-90). The place and date of writing remain uncertain, although Alexandria is a likely place. It could have been destined for a Jewish-Christian audience in the great Egyptian seaport or another Diasporan community.

Hebrews makes references to hardships (10:32-34, 12:4) which included the plundering of property but not the shedding of blood. This is by now a familiar theme in the epistles, and we have another example of a New Testament book written at least partially to encourage Christians to stand fast.

These are, however, only sparse references in what is by New Testament standards a sizeable book. Yet throughout the epistle there is a note of urgency, which Julianna Casey in her *NTM* Hebrews commentary (vol. 18) explains as a rhetorical outpouring since this epistle was originally a homily, first delivered orally and then sent around to other communities. Thus Hebrews, too, originated in a pastoral setting.

F. Revelation

The last book of the Christian Bible is called Revelation or the Apocalypse from the Greek word *apokalypsis* meaning revelation. It has always been enormously controversial, usually because Christians at various stages in history have assumed its imagery to apply to their own day and to forecast an imminent end to the world; for example, Father Jorge in Humberto Eco's novel *The Name of the Rose*. As the close of the second Christian millennium approaches, no doubt many ill-informed preachers will jump on the apocalyptic bandwagon. The Apocalypse does predict the end of the world, but it does so in a visionary way. It does not map out the specifics, although it is safe to assume that the author did anticipate an early Parousia. This book is unusual for the Bible. The Hebrew Scriptures contain no apocalyptic book, although Daniel 7-12 is certainly apocalyptic and traces of this type of writing appear in the later prophets, such as Joel. The synoptic gospels have a brief apocalypse (Mark 13:5-37 = Luke 21:8-36 = Matt 24:4-36), and other New Testament passages have apocalyptic overtones, but these references are slight in comparison with the book of Revelation.

Unfortunately, what is too little known is that apocalyptic was a regular literary genre. To isolate the biblical apocalypse is to misunderstand it. The Judaism of the New Testament period produced several apocalypses, including 1-2 Enoch, 2-3 Baruch, 4 Ezra, the Testament of the Twelve Patriarchs, and the Sibylline Oracles. The Early Christians knew of apocalypses attributed to Peter, Paul, Thomas, and Stephen, as well as 5-6 Ezra, the *Shepherd* of Hermas, and the Christian Sibyllines. Some of these antedate the Johannine Apocalypse, some are contemporary, some postdate it, but all prove that the New Testament Apocalypse is the canonical example of a standard Jewish literary form and not, as the television preachers think, a series of miraculous predictions about the wrath to be visited upon the decadent twentieth century.

The circumstances of the book are clear. Rome, the "whore of Babylon" (chs. 17-18), has become "drunk with the blood of the saints and the blood of the martyrs of Jesus" (17:6). Most scholars date the book *circa* 95 when the emperor Domitian was persecuting the Christians. But Domitian's persecution was not an extensive one, and Christian tradition situates it, like Nero's, only in Rome. On the other hand, local mobs with the approval of Roman officials could incite local persecutions, such as that which took the life of Bishop Polycarp of Smyrna (*ca.* 156), and that may be what occasioned the Apocalypse. Writing about 112, the Roman governor of Bithynia in Asia Minor, Pliny the Younger, brags about the success of a persecution he had initiated and says that he encountered some people who had been Christians but had given up their faith twenty years earlier. If they ceased being Christian because of a persecution, that would put a persecution in Asia Minor in the mid-90s and support the usual date for the Apocalypse.

John, the author, is not the author of the gospel or the three Catholic epistles, so apart from this book he is unknown. He calls himself simply a servant of Jesus Christ (1:1), but he has enough authority to recount his visions to seven different churches in the proconsular province of Asia and thus, in effect, to the whole province. Since he avoids even a common title like elder (*presbyteros*) much less apostle or bishop (*episkopos*), his authority must have been personal rather than institutional.

John can offer no immediate consolation to the seven churches (2:1-3:22), but he can assure them that in the end the forces of the Lamb will be victorious, the angels would punish the wicked, and the new Jerusalem would descend from heaven. He, like several others we have encountered, writes to encourage Christians to stand fast no matter what happens. Like Paul, he has been imprisoned for the faith (1:9), so he does not ask others to do more than he. We will never know if they kept the faith, but we do know that John certainly did his best. Far from being wonderful, visions have often been troublesome, and more than one person having them has echoed Isaiah's lament about such a calling (Isaiah 6:5). This strange book, this revelation which, as Martin Luther observed, does not reveal anything, grew out of the mystic experiences of a lonely man in exile on a prison island who feared for the communities he knew and who tried to warn them in time. He does not exaggerate when he calls himself a servant - not only of Christ but of those churches he cared for.

G. *Acts*

The Acts of the Apostles is not last in order in the New Testament nor is it last chronologically, but we will treat it last here because of our definition of the word "pastoral" as applied to the New Testament books. The Christian scriptures were theological writings which were intended for the good of the whole community and which often addressed specific issues. To an extent, Acts is the most pastoral of all the New Testament books because it points undeniably to the future and attempts to get the Christians ready for that future.

The author of Luke also wrote Acts; of that there is no doubt. The place of writing is again uncertain; the fourth-century writer Jerome says Luke wrote it in Rome. Like the gospel, this is dedicated to Theophilus (1:1), and it presumes that he, and thus every reader, knows the first book. Luke was not an eyewitness to the events of the gospel, but the so-called "we sections" of Acts indicate that he travelled for a while with Paul and witnessed much of what he wrote about and had access to a good source for much of the rest. [Some scholars have suggested that Luke got the "we sections" from someone else's travel diary and was thus not a companion of Paul. Yet all modern scholars agree that Luke was a good theologian as well as a careful and occasionally brilliant writer, so it is difficult to believe that he would suddenly and confusingly switch from the third person to the first on the basis of someone else's diary without a word of explanation.] Although Luke deals with Peter and James and John, his real hero and the central figure of two-thirds of the book is Paul. As we saw earlier, Luke shared Paul's universalist views and put them in his gospel. In this work also, written between 80 and 90, those views are even more prominent.

Before we look at Luke's views, we must consider what the first-time reader of Acts would unquestionably find very odd. The reader learns in any introduction to the book that it was written fifteen to twenty-five years after Paul's death in the mid-60s. Yet Luke carries Paul's story only down to his arrival in Rome *circa* 62. Why did Luke not include an account of Paul's death, especially if he met the glorious death of a martyr? Luke certainly would have known about it, so why does he omit it? A second point which might confuse a first-time reader, especially one who has read the Pauline epistles, is that while the Paul of the epistles expects an imminent Parousia (1 Thes 4:13-5:11, 1 Cor 7:29-31), at least early in his career, Luke's Paul has no concern with it at all.

These two oddities are actually related. Although Luke recorded the synoptic apocalypse (21:8-36), he apparently had little belief in an imminent Parousia. Acts is filled with the theme of continuity between the age of Jesus and that of the apostles. It opens with the same dedication as the gospel, and it repeats the event, the Ascension, which closed the gospel (Luke 24:50-51, Acts 1:6-11). Jesus is gone but his Spirit is with the community, so much so that his disciples perform signs similar to those he performed, such as healing (3:1-10). Like the innocent Jesus, the innocent disciples go before the Jewish authorities (4:1-31, 5:12-42). Luke's description of the centurion Cornelius, who gave liberally to the people (Acts 10:2), recalls the centurion whose servant Jesus healed, "for he loves our (the Jewish) nation, and he built us our synagogue" (Luke 7:6). Luke had the great insight that the world was not going to end immediately and that the Church would be around for some indeterminate time. He thus carries his story past the Resurrection and the initial experiences of the community into an open future. He did not see this as something negative, as a failure of the original revelation, but as a part of God's plan, guided by the Holy Spirit, to get the message to the Gentiles.

Did Luke expect the Church to be around for another 1900 years? Probably not, but after all, how many of us can envision the Church in the 39th. century? But he did expect it to be on earth at least for some time, and he correctly realized that it would have to live with and in the Roman Empire. John the apocalyptist may have expected the imminent fall of Rome, but Luke knew better. In the 60s Rome had fought two fierce wars on either end of the Empire, one against the British in 61 and the other against the Jews from 66 to 70. Rome won both. Only an apocalytist could expect an early end to the Empire.

Now his failure to mention Paul's death makes sense. Luke certainly abhorred what Nero had done to the Christians, but many Romans were also alienated by it. Indeed, Nero's last years had been a series of scandals and vices and murders which provoked assassinations attempts and finally revolts which overthrew him and ushered in civil wars. Luke separated Rome from Nero, and he believed that the Christian message was for everyone, Romans included. He opens Acts in a frontier province, noted for its particularism, but finishes it when his universalist hero has brought his universalist message to the center of the world. The Jews repeatedly reject Paul, who then takes his message to the Gentiles, who are more receptive. The Gentiles are usually Asian Greeks, but good Romans appear, if not as believers like Cornelius, then as rescuers of Paul (18:1-17, 19:21-41, 21: 30-32).

Let us look at one example of Luke's skill in getting this message across. In Acts 25-26 Paul is on trial before the Roman governor Festus. Paul gives a vigorous defence of himself, but, trusting in Roman justice, he declares his wish to be tried by Caesar. Festus says, "You have appealed to Caesar; to Caesar you shall go" (25:12). Shortly thereafter, Festus invites the Jewish puppet-king Herod Agrippa II and his sister Berenice to hear Paul. Paul satisfactorily proves his innocence before them, and Agrippa remarks to the Roman that if Paul had not appealed to Caesar, he could have been released. At first sight, the reader thinks that Paul has made a gross mistake, that if he had only kept his mouth shut he would have been released. But on second thought we realize that the Spirit has been guiding all this, and what appears to be a human error in judgment has been part of a divine plan. The apostle of the new world religion will now go to the capital of the world.

History has vindicated Luke's vision. The Parousia did not occur, and the Roman Empire lasted for another four centuries in the West and another fourteen centuries in the East. After much difficulty, Empire and Church came to live in peace. The Christians who shared Luke's vision were ready for this new world. This is why Acts is so pastoral a book. Luke called the Church to realize its own ongoing existence and its obligation to the world and the presence of God's Spirit as a constant aid. What more could a Christian have done for his brethren?

4

FROM BOOKS TO TESTAMENT: THE CANON

By *circa* 125 all the books of the New Testament had been written, but there was no New Testament because there was no recognized collection of specific Christian books which enjoyed the same status as the Old Testament. The road from the books to the testament was long, bumpy, and lacking signs. In this chapter we will see how the Christians travelled it.

The Old Testament books had great authority for the early Christians, and when Christian writings began to acquire equal stature with the older scriptures, they likewise took on authority. Authority in the early Church requires a separate book, but we cannot treat the question of the canon apart from an understanding of the term authority.

In daily speech authority is usually equated with power, the ability to coerce people into doing something whether they want to or not. But power is external. A lunatic with a weapon can have power over defenceless people. Authority, on the other hand, is internal. One has authority by virtue of knowledge or achievement or respect won from others. It is possible for someone who has authority to have power also: "And they were amazed and said to one another, 'What is this word? For with authority (Greek: *exousia*) and power

(Greek: *dynamis*) he (Jesus) commands the unclean spirits and they come out' " (Luke 4:36).

But power is not at the heart of Jesus' ministry. Mark 1:22: "And they were astonished at his teaching, for he taught them as one who had authority (*exousia*), and not as the scribes." John's gospel even portrays Jesus as refusing to use power even though he could have; "My kingship is not of this world; if my kingship were of this world, my servants would fight that I might not be handed over to the Jews; but my kingship is not of this world" (18:36). Jesus' goals were not those of an earthly king, so he did not use the earthly methods familiar to Pontius Pilate.

We can close this brief discussion with modern examples. Mother Teresa has no power but great authority; the Polish secret police have great power but no authority.

I. The New Testament Evidence

A. The Earliest Authorities

The Christians were never without authority. First, there was the Old Testament, revered by all Jews, including Jesus, and therefore revered by all Christians. They also had the authority of Jesus in his historical person, his resurrected person, and his teaching. It would never have crossed the minds of the first Christians that there could be any conflict between Jesus and the Old Testament since both were from God for the salvation of sinful humanity. They could never be separated. But there was more than this. The Christians read the Hebrew scriptures with a new vision. The history of Israel pointed to Jesus. To look at one without the other was to misunderstand both. This is an important point to remember. Too often we think of the New Testament as the Christian scriptures to be joined to the Jewish scriptures. We should, of course, recognize the independence and validity of the Hebrew Scriptures for Jews, but we must realize that the first Christians did not compose the New Testament books as a Christian Scripture. There was no need to do so because there already was a Christian Bible, the Old Testament read in the light of Christ.

But if the authority of Jesus complemented that of the Hebrew Scriptures, it was also greater. Jesus possessed a unique authority given him by the Father. He could even qualify the Law (Mark 2:23-3:6). His authority was once and for all, and it died with him. But the New Testament does show that has authority could be delegated. Jesus sends out the seventy disciples to evangelize in his name (Luke 10:1-16), and after the resurrection, he commissions his disciples to evangelize the entire world, even to the ends of the earth (Matt 28:16-20). Luke writes that after the ascension, Jesus sent the Holy Spirit to the Twelve, and Luke quickly has Peter perform a sign of healing (Acts 3:1-8) similar to Jesus' signs (for example, Luke 5:17-36) to emphasize both the continuity and validity of the apostolic authority. Peter naturally does not perform miracles in his own name but in the name of Jesus, but the reader does not miss Luke's point.

As the "inner circle," the reconstituted Twelve too had a unique authority, although it was not necessarily superior to other forms. Luke mentions Christian prophets (Acts 11:27, 13:1, 15:32, 21:9) who would also have possessed the Spirit, although not in the same way as the Twelve. But it would not occur to Luke that these two authorities could clash.

In the first decades of Christianity, someone else had a strong view of authority. Paul constantly emphasized his apostolic commission from God (Rom 1:1, 1 Coir 1:1, 2 Cor 1:1, Gal 1:1), and he firmly believed that his calling gave him the right to stand up to members of the Twelve and to James of Jerusalem if they wandered from the straight path (Gal 2). Paul was willing to see the Spirit at work in many Christian ministries, but he could not refrain from ranking the Spirit's gifts, a questionable procedure at best, and we are hardly surprised at the rankings. "And God has appointed in the church first apostles, second prophets, third teachers, then workers or miracles, then healers, helpers, administrators, speakers in various kinds of tongues" (1 Cor 12:28). The important point is clear. There was a concept of authority vested in certain ministries not because they were "officially" designated by a hierarchical structure but because "God has appointed (them) in the church."

The first Christians soon found authority not only in the Old Testament and in prominent individuals but also in the words of Jesus or words of the Lord, as they were often called. The believers passed them along orally in their communities, and eventually some of these words found their way into the gospels or other works, for example, Acts 20:35 and 1 Thess 4:15. Earlier we saw how the sayings were passed along, and how the demands of proclaiming and teaching altered their mode of presentation, freed some from their original narrative setting, and eventually caused some to be preserved and others to disappear. These words of Jesus would carry his unique authority, and in situations where they were particularly applicable, they would have been decisively normative. For example, if a Christian wondered if a people not of this world should pay taxes, Mark 12:7 (= Luke 20:25 = Matt 22:21), "Render to Caesar the things that are Caesar's," would have settled the question, regardless of the views of apostles, prophets, teachers, speakers in tongues, and the like.

It is natural to think that Mark put an end to all this diversity by committing some of Jesus' words to writing and thus starting the shift to written authority in Christianity, but Paul's entire career transpired before Mark wrote a word, and if we look at his epistles we can see some early notions of a written authority. Mark did not step into a complete vacuum.

B. Paul

Paul certainly did not think of his epistles as equal to the Old Testament books, and he clearly preferred to be on the scene himself (1 Thess 3:6. 1 Cor 16:5-7, 2 Cor 1:16). Were that impossible, he would send a trusted disciple (1 Thess 3:1-12) or get information from local contacts (1 Cor 1:11).

Frequently, however, he had to write, and he was well aware that his letters occasionally produced better results than he would have in person (2 Cor 10:9-10). But the letters were more than an effective means of presentation. For Paul, they carried his apostolic authority.

Although specific situations often occasioned Paul's letters, he did not write them hastily or lightly. He weighs his words carefully and argues his point well. He realizes that he cannot be with the recipients, so his authority would stand or fall with his written expressions. He often begins with his apostolic calling to express his individuality (Gal 1:1, 1 Cor 1:1); he includes liturgical formulations to show himself a man of the community (1 Cor 15:3-7, Phil 2:6-11); he insists that he preaches only Christ (1 Cor 2:2); when he addresses novel situations, he gives "(his) opinion as one who by the Lord's mercy is trustworthy" (1 Cor 7:25). When one of his letters backfires (2 Cor 2:4), he is astonished. Paul's letters represent Paul; to question them is to question his divine commission. Paul apparently made this point stick because even in the New Testament there is evidence of his letters taking on the authority of a sacred collection.

Anything written takes on a life of its own, independent of the writer. Paul may have written for specific occasions, but he was an apostle of God, and the communities which received his letters were likely to hold on to them, to copy them, circulate them, and later to treasure them. At some point it occurred to someone to collect Paul's letters. He or she did it before 125 since 2 Peter 3:15-16 presumes such a collection. Did Paul do it? An assistant? A disciple? We could answer that question better if we could be sure who wrote the epistles to the Colossians and the Ephesians.

Colossians 4:16 says, "And when this letter has been read among you, have it read also in the church of the Laodiceans, and see that you read also the letter from Laodicea." If, as is likely, Paul wrote Colossians and thus also Laodiceans, he here demonstrates an awareness that his letters have more than immediate importance. He expects communities to exchange them and to read them publicly (liturgically?). Thus Paul would be encouraging a formal treatment of his letters, and a collection was inevitable since each Pauline foundation would want all the letters. On the other hand, if Paul did not write Colossians, the implication is that a collection has already begun, and pseudonymous author wants his letter passed about so that it would join the others as Pauline.

As mentioned earlier, many scholars consider Ephesians a general introduction to the Pauline letters. If Paul wrote an introduction to a collection of his own works, he either made the collection or directed it or, at the very least, gave it his approval. If someone else wrote Ephesians, then we cannot be sure if he made the collection or wrote an introduction to an already existing body of letters. These theories also presume that Ephesians is indeed an introduction to such a collection, and that is not a unanimously accepted proposition.

It is likely that Paul, with his confidence in his apostolic calling, realized that his letters were significant documents. Whether he wrote Colossians or Ephesians or not, his own attitude would have been the impetus behind an early collection of his letters. Since he probably kept copies of these letters, he is the best candidate for initiating such a collection.

One final note about Paul. He is the only New Testament author to use the word "canon" (Greek: *kanon*). In Galatians 6:16 he says "Peace and mercy be upon all who walk by this rule (*kanon*), upon the Israel of God." Canon originally meant a hollow reed which was used for a measuring rod and by extension came to mean a rule, much the way a yardstick is a physical measuring device as well as a term for measuring non-physical things such as economic progress. (This Greek word for hollow reed also forms the basis of the word cannon.) When we speak of a book's being in the canon, we mean that it belongs to the list of scriptural books, but in the earliest church the word canon also meant the measure of the Church's faith and practice. When the canon as list was being determined, no one used the word to mean just a list. The books made it onto the list because they were "canonical," that is, they suited the Church's faith and practice.

C. The Gospels

We turn now to Mark's gospel, the earliest known written record of Jesus' words. The importance of this book for the canon cannot be overestimated. For four decades the Christians had passed along Jesus' words, shading and adapting them to various situations with the inevitable result that the words themselves changed. Mark put a halt to that process. He did not preserve the authentic words of Jesus from corruption. What he did do was preserve the traditions he knew by giving them the permanence of writing. He also gave those traditions an authority they had not previously possessed.

We saw in the last chapter that the written words eventually replaced the oral traditions. This probably was not Mark's original goal, but it happened almost inevitably since people seem to prefer permanent records. ("Be sure to get it in writing!") Once the written record replaced the oral, it became the locus, or place, of authority. Mark's gospel had authority because it included the words (and deeds) of Jesus. But as it became identified as the source for these, its authority began to replace theirs. The sequence was: Jesus' words › Jesus' words as preserved in the gospel › the gospel.

Once this process had begun, it could not be reversed. The gospels of Luke and Matthew, clearly following the Markan pattern, accelerated the decline of oral traditions. John's gospel may have been originally the possession of a separatist community, but once it became widely known and was thought to be the work of a disciple special to Jesus, it too took on great authority. Mark, Luke, and Matthew probably did not consider their books to be on a par with the Old Testament writings, but as their gospels became valued as sources for the knowledge of Jesus, through whom the Old Testament had to be read, the authority previously given to

Jesus' words and deeds and to the Old Testament slowly became theirs. The redactor of John's gospel probably considered the testimony of the Beloved Disciple to be the equivalent of a revelation from the Spirit in light of the Disciple's normative role for the community, but exact words to that effect do not appear in the gospel itself.

It took a while for the gospels to be considered a group, and the first evidence for it appears in the mid-second century. This is understandable because unlike the Pauline epistles, the gospels emerged from four pens and four communities, and apparently there were more than four documents to choose from even at an early date (Luke 1:1).

D. Revelation and the Non-Pauline Epistles

The growing corpus of Christian writings spurred other authors to write, including the visionary and prophet John, who never doubted that he was under the Spirit's influence. His warning to his readers not to change one word of his text under threat of divine retribution proves this (22:18-19). John could not write for a canon since there was no canon *circa* 95, but he is the only New Testament author to claim openly inspiration of the Spirit not just for himself but for his book. The Old Testament books could not claim more.

Another element in the New Testament which points to a consciousness of canonicity is the increasing awareness of the Old Testament canon. Even in Judaism at this time the canon of the Old Testament was not completely defined; that awaited the rabbinical council at Jamnia *circa* 90, and the authority and even the existence of that council are debated. The Christian canon of the Old Testament was equally uncertain, but this uncertainty applied only to a few books such as Ruth, Lamentations, the Song of Songs, and Esther, The basic canon, that is, the Pentateuch, the historical books, the major and minor prophets, and the "Writings," such as the Psalms, was settled. There are several references in the New Testament to the Law, the Law and the prophets (Matt 5:17, 7:12; Luke 16:16), and once to "the

Law of Moses and the prophets and the psalms" (Luke 24:44).

Outside the canonical and the debated books were numerous apocryphal works which were widely circulated and read but with little or no chance of entering the canon. These books have survived in a number of ways, including preservation at Qumran, and they considerably influenced the New Testament writers, an influence which scholars are investigating more and more. Paul knew these apocrypha, and he alluded to one in 1 Cor 10:4, the account of the rock which followed the Israelites in the desert. This was most likely a rabbinic legend. The author of Hebrews refers to the harsh fates of the Hebrew prophets, which included being sawn in half (11:37), the fate of Isaiah at the hands of Manasseh not according to any canonical book but according to the Ascension of Isaiah, an apocryphon of the first century B.C. John 4:14 refers to water "welling up" to eternal life in Jacob's well. That phrase appears in a Jewish tradition about Jacob's removal of a stone from the head of the well.

Unlike Paul, John, and the author of Hebrews, "Jude" does not make occasional allusions to apocrypha but rather fills his short letter with references and details taken from them, for example, the disobedient angels in chains (v. 6) and the dispute between the archangel Michael and Satan over the body of Moses (v. 9). In v. 14 Jude openly quotes 1 Enoch. This brief epistle testifies to the openness of some Christians to non-canonical literature.

By the time 2 Peter was written this openness to the apocrypha had become embarrassing. Jesus is dead almost a century, and the church had become settled. Order and organization were necessary for the growing number of communities. One element in this new situation was a tightening up of which books were to be used as authoritative in the community. (This was not an early form of ecclesiastical censorship. The question was not whether the books should be read by those who wished to read them but rather what authority the community should give them.)

2 Peter 2:1-22 effectively rewrote Jude 4-16, preserving much of the language and imagery but excising all the apocryphal material. If the Christians had become conscious of what did or did not belong in the Old Testament and what was thus proper for citation in Christian works, could an awareness of what were the truly Christian books be far behind?

2 Peter provides an idea of which book had already gained some acceptance. One apparently was Jude since he goes to such pains to fix it up. The others are the Pauline epistles. "So also our brother Paul wrote to you according to the wisdom given him, speaking of this as he does in all his letters. There are some things in them hard to understand, which the ignorant and unstable twist to their own destruction, as they do the other Scriptures" (3:15-16) Significantly Peter refers to "all his letters," implying a collection, although with no indication of which epistles might be in it. "The ignorant and the unstable" - probably the false teachers attacked in ch. 2 - twist Paul's words, suggesting some kind of exegesis or public disputation about Paul's meaning. Finally, there is that striking phrase "as they do the other Scriptures," here using the plural of the Greek *graphe*, the usual New Testament term for the Old Testament. How does Peter mean that? Were Paul's works to be accepted on a par with the Old Testament books? If so, how? There was no formal New Testament canon for the Pauline epistles to join, and they certainly did not belong in the Old Testament. They could not form an independent canon; Peter's concern with Jude proves that. And what about 1 Peter which this author knew (2 Peter 3:1)? Finally, any collection of Christian books would have to have at least one account of Jesus' life and teachings, that is, a gospel. The best we can say is that some Christians, represented at least by "Peter" and the communities to which he wrote, were moving in the direction of a New Testament canon.

II. The Patristic Evidence

A. Scripture and Patristics

Patristics is the study of the Church Fathers (Latin: *patres*), the writers and theologians who shaped Christianity in its formative period from the apostolic age to approximately the fifth or sixth century. The Fathers include great and famous names like John Chrysostom, Ambrose, Basil the Great, and Augustine, and the patristic period gave us the basic Christian teachings on the Trinity (a word which does not even appear in the New Testament) and the person of Christ. In general, the Fathers came later than the New Testament writers, and patristics is often a separate area of study. But this scholarly division in no way reflects the actual historical situation; there was no point at which a voice from a cloud announced to the Christians that the New Testament period had ended and the patristic era had begun. Indeed, for the earliest Fathers, there is considerable overlapping. Clement of Rome wrote his *First Epistle to the Corinthians circa* 95, thus making it contemporary with the Apocalypse, James, and 1 Peter, just before the Johannine writings, and definitely earlier than the three Pastorals and 2 Peter. Ignatius of Antioch wrote his seven epistles *circa* 110-115, making them contemporaries of the Pastorals and earlier than 2 Peter. The pseudonymous *Epistle of Barnabas* has been dated as early as 70, which would make it as old or older than all the New Testament literature except the Pauline epistles; the majority of scholars, however, favor a date *circa* 130, which means it is at least contemporary with 2 Peter. That scriptural epistle's late date also makes it a contemporary of the first Christian apologist, Quadratus, and of the homily known as Clement's *Second Epistle to the Corinthians.* Some scholars, including the influential Hans von Campenhausen, would date the Pastorals *circa* 150, a date which some few others have suggested for the Acts of the Apostles. If these speculations were correct, some New Testament works would postdate several patristic works, including all the ones just mentioned plus the early work of

Justin Martyr, the visionary *Shepherd* of Hermas, and Polycarp's *Epistle to the Philippians*. These are definitely minority views, but they serve to illustrate how uncertain the dating of New Testament books can be. Even the conservative, widely-accepted dates prove that chronological priority does not separate patristic from New Testament because not all the scriptural books are chronologically prior to the patristic books.

This situation is true not only for the traditional Fathers, that is, those writers whom later generations deemed founders of Christian teaching and practice, but also for the Gnostics, labelled "heretics" by earlier generations. Today we recognize that many Fathers taught notions which later generations would consider heretical, and some unquestioned Fathers, such as Tertullian, left the larger Church for an heretical sect and even founded their own sects. Modern scholars usually avoid the term "heresy," and patristics now includes the study of the Gnostics, a catch-all term applied to various sects united mostly by their claims to a special revelation or knowledge (Greek: *gnosis*) and by opposition to and from the larger or catholic Church. (This is not equivalent with the Roman Catholic Church but means the universal church as opposed to particularist sects.) The discovery of Gnostic books at Nag Hammadi in Egypt has enhanced the study of the Gnostic movement, which now appears a creative if somewhat exclusivist force in Early Christianity. Some Gnostic writings date back to the early second century and are contemporaneous with the later New Testament works, but scholars have claimed that elements in Gnostic writings go back to the first century. Chronology simply cannot be the dividing line between the scriptural and non-scriptural books.

Is not then canonicity the dividing line between New Testament and patristic? Twenty-seven books are in the New Testament, and the others simply are not. That is true today, but such a statement is meaningless for the late first and early second centuries. There existed no canon from which the patristic texts were excluded. No one living then knew the difference between a scriptural writer and a

Church Father. In this period several Christians wrote books for a variety of reasons, usually pastoral. Later generations discerned the scriptural or canonical status of twenty-seven of them. Maybe some particularly prescient Christian *circa* 100 read Luke's gospel and Clement's epistle and concluded that the former was on a par with the Old Testament and the latter was not, but the available evidence shows much uncertainty on this question. There were no formal literary or theological principles for establishing a canon of Christian writings. The New Testament, like its individual books, came into being in the lived experience of the Church. Only slowly and with difficulty was it distinguished from the writings of the Fathers.

B. The Earliest Fathers

The earliest Father, Clement of Rome, wrote to the Church at Corinth *circa* 95 because a dispute there had rent the community into factions, a situation reminiscent of Paul's day. Clement wrote a fraternal letter on behalf of the Church of Rome, and he did not use his own name. [His authorship is known from a later source.] He tries to call the Corinthians back to harmony with a variety of arguments taken mostly from the Septuagint verson of the Old Testament. But Clement also cites the epistles of Paul, such as Philippians and 1 Corinthians (ch. 47), and, although not by name, the epistle to the Hebrews (ch. 36). Of particular interest is ch. 46 where Clement says, "It is written: 'Cling to the saints, for they who cling to them will become saints'." The source of this saying is unknown. It is not scriptural, but he uses the customary Early Christian formula for citing Scripture, "it is written" (cf. Matt 11:1, Luke 3:4, John 2:17, Rom 4:17, Gal 3:10). The saying may be from an apocryphal book considered authoritative in Clement's day or at least in his community. He goes on: "Remember the words of the Lord Jesus, for he said, 'Woe to that man! It were better for him if he had not been born, rather than to scandalize one of my elect. It would be better for him to be girded with a millstone and to be drowned in the sea than to pervert one of my chosen ones'." This sounds very scriptural, but it is nowhere found in the gospels in this form. It is an amalgam of several independent verses: Matt 18:6, 26:24; Mark 9:42; Luke 17:2, 22:22. Did Clement take the verses from the written gospels and put them into this form? Was he citing an oral saying not preserved in the canonical gospels? Was he citing a written book similar to our gospels but which has not survived? There is no way to tell in this passage or in some others just what Clement actually was citing; probably he knew both oral and written traditions about Jesus. No matter what the answer, we can see that just because there were written gospels, not all Christians used only them to learn about Jesus. For the first generations, the words and deeds of Jesus were more important than the sources preserving them.

Clement also indicates (ch. 42) that for him the age of the apostles is over. Such an attitude will further the idea of a New Testament when the supposedly apostolic books are seen as relics of the bygone age, but at this early stage there is no link yet between the age and the books.

Ignatius of Antioch, a martyr-bishop who was thrown to the lions at Rome, took very much the same attitude, but he still strongly advanced the process of canonization. On his way as a prisoner to Rome (*circa* 115), he wrote seven letters, one each to the Christian communities at Smyrna, Ephesus, Philadelphia, Magnesia, Tralles, and Rome, and one to Bishop Polycarp of Smyrna. In these he cites or alludes to several New Testament books. Ignatius knows most Pauline epistles: Romans, 1 Corinthians, Galatians, Philippians, Colossians, and 1 Thessalonians, as well as Ephesians. [From here on we will include Ephesians among the Pauline epistles since the writers of Christian Antiquity considered it such.] He may have known John's gospel, but it is equally possible that he actually knew the author. He may have known 1 Peter. There is no way to tell if he knew the synoptics or oral traditions about Jesus. He cites these words of Jesus to Peter and the others: "Take, handle me and see that I am not a bodiless demon" (*Smyrneans* 3), a passage reminiscent of Luke 24:39 and John 20:24-29. But the first scriptural passage deals with an appearance to all the Eleven and the second with the doubting Thomas; neither deals with Peter. Ignatius regards this apocryphal saying as the word of the Lord, so he obviously used books outside our New Testament. Yet he does not cite any of these sources as scripture. The authority of Paul stands behind the epistles and the sayings of Jesus give authority to the gospels and similar works, but there is still no question of a canon.

In spite of this, Ignatius did affect the canon because he raised the question of authority in the Church. His letters show that there were three basic Christian parties at Antioch: a middle party headed by him, an ultra-conservative Judaizing party intent on having Christians adhere to Jewish regulations, and an ultra-liberal party, most likely converted pagans, who could not accept the idea that the Son of God had taken on corruptible flesh and who thus claimed that Jesus only seemed to have a body. The Judaizers prove how one-sided is the view of the Church we get from Acts. Antioch was Paul's base for his missionary journeys, yet a sizeable group there could still reject his life's work. The other group, called Docetists (from the Greek verb *dokeo*, to seem) was known outside Antioch (John 1:14; 1 John 4:2); it is a good example of what can happen to a religion established in one culture, in this case, Semitic, and transferred to another, in this case, Hellenistic.

Ignatius had been unable to win over either group, so he resorted to what was then a new tactic. He insisted upon the bishop (Greek: *episkopos*) as the source of unity in the congregation, and he argued that there was no true community without the bishop (*Smyrneans* 8, *Philadelphians* 4, *Trallians* 2-3, *Ephesians* 7). Although there are hints elsewhere of hierarchical authority, for example, 3 John 9-10 (the word *episkopos* is not used there), there was nothing like this. *Episkopos* originally meant overseer, and it is not an especially hierarchical term as used in the New Testament (cf. Acts 1:20, 20:17, 28; 1 Peter 2:25). The *episkopoi* are distinct from the *diakonoi* but not always from the *presbyteroi.* Clement of Rome, in papal tradition the third successor of Peter as *episkopos* of Rome, did not write in his own name - he did not even mention it - but wrote for "the church of God which dwells as a pilgrim in Rome"(ch. 1). In ch. 44 of his letter he uses the terms *episkopos* and *presbyteros* interchangeably, and many modern scholars favor the term presbyter-bishop for this time period.

No one can say what prompted Ignatius to emphasize the authority of the bishop's office; most likely the divisive situation at Antioch forced him to try this. Inadvertently he initiated what became a regular feature of church life in the second century and survives today. The bishop's office became distinct from the priest's, and increasingly the bishop, who was usually elected by his congregation, represented and spoke for the congregation. The problems of heterodoxy and schism had shown the need for a new locus of authority. More and more communities relied upon a bishop, but the search for reliable authority would also go in another direction - toward the New Testament.

Ignatius' emphasis on the bishop's office reveals something else. For him, as for Clement, the apostolic age is over (*Magnesians* 13, *Trallians* 2, *Smyrneans* 8). Ignatius draws the conclusion that there must still be living authority in the Church, and he sees the bishop filling that role. But why not the words of Jesus? The answer is probably that the dissidents could twist those words to their own meaning (as "Peter" claimed the "ignorant and unstable" had done to Paul's words; cf. 2 Peter 3:16), and we have a good example of what could have happened, although it dates about twenty or thirty years after Ignatius.

The crucifixion of Jesus bothered many Christians, such as the author of John's gospel, and some like the Docetists sought to deny that it ever happened, for example, Jesus only seemed to have a body, so this phantom body was not really crucified. The Church Father Irenaeus, writing *circa* 180, tells of the Gnostic Basilides, who went a step further than the Docetists. He taught that Jesus was an incorporeal power who could change his body as he pleased, so on the road to Calvary he switched bodies with Simon of Cyrene, who was then crucified in his place. While Simon hung in agony on the cross, Jesus (in Simon's body) laughed at how he had deceived his would-be executioners. To us this sounds ridiculous as well as completely un-Christian, but it demonstrates what some people in the second century could do to Christian teaching. Ignatius' solution to the problem may not have been the best, but he had to do something.

Ignatius may have affected the canon in another, almost fascinating way. On his journey to Rome he met with Onesimus, bishop of Ephesus at Smyrna (*Ephesians* 1). Christian tradition identified this man with the runaway slave who occasioned Paul's letter to Philemon, something physically possible if Onesimus had been young in Paul's day. Modern scholarship has been skeptical of this identification, but the American scholar John Knox defended it forty years ago, and another American, William Farmer, has revived it. The identification is attractive because it explains a real problem of the canon, that is, how was a purely personal letter by Paul preserved. Onesimus obviously had a great personal interest in it - he had been the occasion of a letter by the great apostle to the Gentiles - and his position as bishop of Ephesus would allow him to give the letter some public exposure. The host of Ignatius and Onesimus at Smyrna was Polycarp, an important martyr-bishop, author of a letter to the Philippians and a visitor to Rome. If this meeting had made him and Ignatius aware of this precious little Pauline letter, they could have become agents in its dissemination. This is just a hypothesis, but a good one.

The evidence after Ignatius is spotty and inconclusive, but some New Testament books are obviously gaining in authority. Polycarp (d. *ca.* 155) definitely knew of a Pauline collection and cites or alludes to Romans, 1 Corinthians, Galatians, Ephesians, Philippians, Colossians, 2 Thessalonians, 1-2 Timothy (usually considered Pauline down to the twentieth century), and possibly 2 Corinthians. He also knew Hebrews, 1 Peter, Matthew, and possibly 1 or 2 John. Since all these references appear in one brief epistle (nine pages in English), Polycarp is an invaluable source for Paul's influence in Asia Minor at least. But Paul is not yet scripture. The "word of truth" (*Philippians* 3) can be transmitted orally or in writing.

The *Didache*, contemporary with Polycarp in its written form but based on much older material, uses the formula "The Lord directed in his gospel" (8:2) to preface a version of the Lord's Prayer which is close to Matthew's version (6:9-13). The Didachist knew both Matthew and oral traditions. Equally indecisive is the pseudonymous *Epistle of Barnabas*, whose author uses the phrase "it is written" (4:4) for a citation of Matthew 22:14. Ironically, in that same chapter (4:3) he cites by name the Book of Enoch. He also cites the apocryphal 2 Baruch (11:9) and 2 Esdras (12:1) as the works of prophets. Matthew may be scriptural, but for "Barnabas" so are these apocryphal works.

The homily known as the *Second Epistle to the Corinthians* and pseudonymously attributed to Clement of Rome, dates *circa* 130 and is possibly from Rome. It uses the word "scripture" (Greek: *graphe*) for the gospel. 2 Clement 2:4 reads: "Another scripture says, 'I have come not to call the just but sinners' " (Matt 9:13). This is the first time in history that the word *graphe*, the standard Christian term for the Old Testament - and used as such in 2 Clement 6:8 and 14:2 - is applied to a New Testament book.

This sounds like a real breakthrough until we look at 2 Clement 8:5: "For the Lord says in the gospel, 'If you do not keep what is small, who will give you what is great? For I say to you, that he who is faithful in that which is least is faithful also in that which is great'." This reflects Luke 16:10-12, but it appears in none of the extant gospels. It derives either from an oral tradition or an apocryphal gospel. Furthermore, 2 Clement 5:2 has an openly apocryphal citation: "For the Lord said, 'You shall be as lambs in the midst of wolves'." The gospels were growing in authority, but what kind of authority is debatable.

C. The Apologists

In the middle of the second century a new type of Christian literature emerged, apologetics. The apologists tried to present a reasoned defence of the Christian position to the outside world and thus composed the first Christian writings aimed primarily at non-Christians. The apologists' techniques differed from those of the earlier writers, since they could not impress pagans with citations from the Old Testament, but there are occasional references in their writings which show the progress of the New Testament. The most important apologist is Justin Martyr (d. *ca.* 165). He refers to "the memoirs of the apostles" (1 *Apology* 67:3) which were read liturgically and had been for some time. Justin also knows of "gospels;" earlier writers had spoken only of "the gospel," a phrase which Justin also uses (*Dialogue with Trypho* 10:2, 100:1). He quotes John's gospel only once (John 3:3 in 1 *Apology* 61:4), but he does know it. He cites all the synoptics, including a Markan passage not paralleled in Luke or Matthew (Mark 3:17 in *Dialogue* 106). He also cites sayings of Jesus which do not appear in the gospels, but are at least partially composed from an apocryphon and the synoptics. He cites Pauline passages, but never mentions Paul. It appears that Justin acknowledged the unique authority of the four gospels but not to the exclusion of other sources for the words of Jesus.

This not-so-complete uniqueness of the four gospels appears in a remarkable way in the work of Tatian the Syrian (*fl. ca.* 160-175), a pupil of Justin. He composed a continuous gospel narrative called in Greek the *Diatessaron*, literally, "through the four." Tatian's Syriac version was so popular that it was read liturgically in Syria until the fifth century when the canonical gospels finally replaced it. The *Diatessaron* well illustrates the Christian ambivalence on the gospels: Tatian accepts the authority of the four, no more or less, but he feels perfectly free to use them to create a completely new work of his own.

D. Marcion

The person who put an end to the ambivalence and produced the first formal New Testament canon was Marcion, a ship-builder from Pontus on the southern shore of the Black Sea and, according to his many opponents (Justin, Irenaeus, and Tertullian among others), the worst heretic in history. Modern scholars have been far more lenient and occasionally quite favorable to him.

Marcion is one of those historical figures known only from what his opponents said of him. Almost every aspect of his career is debated, but in general it was this. He was the son of a bishop in Asia Minor, but his father excommunicated him for his unorthodox views. His commercial success enabled him to travel, and *circa* 140 he went to Rome where he was accepted into the Christian community, to which he gave a considerable financial gift. In 144 the community excommunicated him and returned his money. He then set himself to the task of founding a network of churches in the Eastern half of the Mediterranean. These communities largely disappeared in the third century, although some survived into the fourth and fifth.

What were these views which caused such a stir?

Marcion could not reconcile the just God of the Old Testament, the Creator God who produced the world of matter, and the good but unknown God of the Christians. He concluded that there must be two gods. Since the Creator God, the opposite of the good God, was the god of the Jews, Marcion rejected the Jewish Bible. To replace it, he created a new one.

Marcion believed that Jesus had brought liberation from the Law imposed by the Creator God upon the Jews, but Jesus' Jewish disciples had inevitably if not deliberately perverted his message. Paul saw through all this, and he emphasized grace over law. Marcion considered Paul's ten epistles (interestingly he did not include the Pastorals) to be canonical scripture. But Paul did not provide an account of Jesus, so for this Marcion turned to the gospel which most reflected Paul's views, namely, Luke. Since Luke's gospel included some Jewish sentiments, Marcion had to expurgate it to get an acceptable gospel. He did not call his work a New Testament because for him there was no Old Testament, just a collection of Jewish regulations and superstitions. He called his work simply Gospel and Apostle. But it was a true New Testament - a fixed collection of Christian writings considered to be divinely inspired scripture and not open to change or alteration.

This clumsy canon reveals Marcion's shallow approach. A Paul who rejects the Old Testament never lived, and a gospel based upon what Marcion acknowledged to be an unacceptable source is not a gospel. He had no idea of development in the concept of God, and he did not appreciate the tension in Paul's writings between the Law and freedom in Christ. But Marcion had done what no one else had. He had raised the question, "Are there scriptures written by Christians?," and he had done so by emphasizing the difference between the Old and New Testaments. Other Christians had noticed it but had tried to understand it by allegory to typology, that is, that the Old Testament passages somehow pointed to a Christian message, but Marcion insisted on a literal or historical approach to the Hebrew scriptures to drive his point home. The catholic Church rejected his rejection of the Old Testament, but the issue could not be easily overlooked. Approximately twenty-five years after Marcion's difficulties in Rome, Melito of Sardis, an orthodox bishop, became the first Christian to use the phrase "the Old Testament" for the Hebrew Scriptures, as reported by the church historian Eusebius of Caesarea (*H.E.* 4, 26, 13). The gap had opened.

Marcion had done more. He showed how one could argue from and with a canon. For example, exclusion of "Jewish" gospels in favor of a "Pauline" one alters the understanding of Jesus. Exclusion of the non-Pauline epistles effectively eliminates all non-Pauline views of the Church. Even his arrangement of the epistles has a particularizing effect. He put Galatians first because in it Paul had stood up to the Judaizers and Peter, traditional founder of the Roman church which had expelled him. [Next came 1-2 Corinthians, Romans, 1-2 Thessalonians, Ephesians (called Laodiceans by Marcion), Colossians, Philemon, and Philippians.] Marcion was the first but not the last person to use Paul for a radical critique of prevailing Christian belief and practice. Pelagius, Luther, and Karl Barth all followed in his footsteps, although for very different reasons.

It is an overstatement to say that Marcion was the first to think of a New Testament canon. As we have seen, other Christians were moving in that direction. But Marcion had radically altered the situation by showing it could be done. Another man was to show that it had to be done.

E. Montanus

In the second century the authority and power of the bishops had grown, largely because of increasing numbers of Christians as well as their diversity and geographical spread. This required more and more organization. A single bishop could act more effectively than a council of presbyters and a great deal more effectively than wandering prophets and speakers in tongues. To some people this development, coupled with the growing reliance on the now unchangeable words of Jesus as preserved in the written gospels, meant an ever-decreasing role for the Spirit. Another second-century development, the rise of the apologists who tried to bridge the gap between Christianity and the world, compromised the apocalyptic tradition of an imminent return of Christ and the destruction of the sinful world. A conservative reaction set in. The Holy Spirit spoke to Montanus.

Montanus (*fl. ca.* 156-157) lived in Phrygia in western Asia Minor. He received revelations from the Holy Spirit and began to prophesy ecstatically that the Heavenly Jerusalem would shortly descend near the little Asian town of Pepuza. Soon two prophetesses joined him, Maximilla and Priscilla. The movement, called the New Prophecy, was initially very popular, and some bishops went along with it because no one wished to be against the Spirit. But the predictions went unfulfilled, and the movement inevitably attracted frauds and charlatans. The organized churches and several orthodox writers began to attack it, and it withered under the criticism. One account (Eusebius *H.E.* 5, 16, 12) reports that Montanus and Maximilla hanged themselves at the collapse of the movement. The New Prophecy briefly survived them, and in the person of Tertullian it enjoyed some success in North Africa in the third century, but it essentially petered out after the death of the prophet although pockets survived until the fourth century.

Like Marcion, Montanus is known mostly from the hostile works of others. A few prophecies survive. Montanus said, "I am the Father and I am the Son and I am the Paraclete." Maximilla said, "Listen not to me but to Christ;" "I am word and spirit and power;" "After me, there will be no more prophets but the consummation." Priscilla said, "In the form of a woman, arrayed in shining garments, came Christ to me and set wisdom upon me and revealed to me that this place (Pepuza) is holy and that Jerusalem will come down from heaven." Montanus and his prophetesses were never accused of willful fraud, but rather of being deluded, and these few quotations show why. The claims were grandiose, and some were simply wrong. In the eyes of most Christians, Montanus was a false prophet. But this false prophet had raised a question which no true prophet could have: how does one tell an authentic revelation from the Spirit?

Montanus' failure was proof to his contemporaries that he did not have the Spirit, but could not that have been determined sooner? The institutional authority of the clergy could not measure up to the authority of the Spirit, so that avenue was closed. But if there were some source which contained the authentic teaching of the Spirit, the truth or validity of a revelation could be checked against it because the Spirit could not be self-contradictory. Like Marcion, Montanus caused the Christians to consider whether there was a collection of Christian books similar to the Old Testament, that is, inspired by the Spirit, and thus a reliable standard for Christian life and teaching. The first use of the Greek phrase *kaine diatheke*, "new covenant," (Latin: *novum testamentum*, and thus English: New Testament) for a collection of books was used by an anonymous, anti-Montanist writer in a passage preserved by Eusebius (*H.E.* 5.16). The anonymous writer does not have a closed collection of books in mind - indeed, he is convinced that his own work could be included in the *kaine diatheke* - and he speaks of "the word of the new covenant" rather than apply the title to the collection, but the term is there, waiting for a third-century author to apply it to the books.

F. Apostolicity and Gnosticism

The best answer to the teachings of Marcion and the prophecies of the Montanists was apostolicity, that is, to insist that any position claiming to be Christian must have a foundation in the teaching of the apostles or their disciples. Some of the apostles' message had been passed along orally, and some of it was preserved in the New Testament books. But use of "apostolic" writings opened up Christianity to attack from yet another quarter. Gnosticism in various forms was flourishing in the second century. Most Gnostics were content to allegorize the Old Testament, and since John's gospel was popular with them, they did not follow Marcion's rampant Paulinism. Teachers who stressed gnosis, secret traditions of knowledge about the cosmos and the interior being, had little sympathy for Montanus' ecstatic revelations. They, too, agreed that the source for Christian authority was apostolicity, and for a good reason. They had a variety of gospels by the apostles - the one by John but also gospels by Thomas, Philip, Jude, James, and Bartholomew among others. (The next chapter will look at these.) To these writings the Gnostics could add secret oral traditions dating back to the apostles. Although the Gnostics relied upon more than just apostolicity for authority, the notion was tailor-made for them. Thus, to combat the Marcionites and Montanists with teachings taken from the apostles and largely preserved in "apostolic" literature, the Church would leave itself wide open to the Gnostic claims.

Rarely has the Church been in such a dilemma, but as in an old Western movie, the cavalry came riding over the hill in the nick of time. The "cavalry" was named Irenaeus of Lyons (*ca.* 130 - *ca.* 200).

G. *Irenaeus of Lyons*

Irenaeus originally lived in Asia Minor, probably Smyrna, since as a boy he heard Polycarp of Smyrna speak. He studied at Rome and later became a presbyter among the heavily Asian congregation at Lyons. He was at Rome to plead for moderation for the Montanists in 177 when a violent persecution broke out at Lyons. The martyrs included the bishop, and upon his return in 178 Irenaeus took over that office. Legend says he too died as a martyr.

Like many great figures of history, Irenaeus was basically conservative, and he would have been astonished at the revolution his works wrought. He feared the Gnostic influence in Christianity, and he tried to ward it off with his *Detection and Overthrow of the Pretended but False Gnosis*, known better and more simply as *Against Heresies* (*A.H.*). It is a wide-ranging book which preserves much valuable information about the Gnostics. It is also poorly organized and often repetitive, but it is the first real Christian theological work since John's gospel. Of greatest importance is its method.

Irenaeus opposed many points in Gnostic teaching, but the Gnostics could claim apostolic authority for them since they had access to secret traditions and books known only to their sects. This put the catholics at a disadvantage since they could not know how many and what kind of traditions the Gnostics could access, nor could they be sure when one of these traditions would surface to support a Gnostic position. It was the great insight of Irenaeus to turn this pillar of Gnostic strength into its chief weakness. His attack was severe and direct:

The tradition of the apostles, made clear in all the world, can be seen in every church by those who wish to behold the truth. We can enumerate those who were established by the apostles as bishops in the churches, and their successors down to our time, none of whom taught or thought of anything like their (the Gnostics') mad ideas. Even if the apostles had known of hidden mysteries, which they taught to the perfect secretly and apart from others, they would have handed them down to those whom they placed in charge of the churches. (*A.H.* 3,3,1)

His reasoning is very persuasive. If a certain teaching were so important, why would the Apostles not have taught it to those in charge of the churches? The catholic party could trace what it taught back to the time of the apostles, a claim the Gnostics could not make. The logical corollary is that if the Gnostics could not clearly trace their teachings back to the apostles, how could they prove their teachings were apostolic and not newly minted? Ironically, even if the Gnostics did have genuine apostolic traditions, they would now have difficulty proving that. Apostolicity, previously a strong point of the Gnostics, had been completely turned against them.

Irenaeus had exposed the weakness of the Gnostics but also of Marcion and Montanus and anyone else claiming to alter the received traditions or introduce new sources. Now he had to produce a reliable method of his own. He agrees with his contemporaries that apostolic teaching should be the only source of authority, and he claims that this source appears in two places. One locus was mentioned in the earlier passage, those churches which could trace their foundations back to the apostles.

Wherefore it is incumbent to obey the presbyters who are in the Church, those who as I have shown possess the succession from the apostles; those who, together with the successors of the episcopate, have received the certain gift of truth, according to the good pleasure of the Father. (*A.H.* 4,26,2)

Later in the book he became more specific, focussing on those churches with a succession of orthodox bishops whom he considered successors of the apostles.

> To enumerate the successions of all the churches would take up too much space in a volume of this kind. But in order to put to shame all of those who in any way, either through self-conceit, or through vain-glory, or through blind and evil opinion, gather as they should not, I need only cite the case of that very great, most ancient and universally known church founded and established at Rome by those two most glorious apostles Peter and Paul and draw attention to the tradition which that church has received from the apostles and to the faith it preaches which has come down to our time through the succession of bishops. (*A.H.* 3,3,2)

He goes on:

> Similarly there was Polycarp, who was not only taught by the apostles and associated with many who had seen the Lord, but also was installed by apostles in Asia as bishop in the church of Smyrna. . . . He too always taught what he learned from the apostles. This is what the Church continues to hand on. This alone is true. (*A.H.* 3,3,4)

This is more than just a glorification of episcopal succession. It recalls the values of the earliest Church which favored direct contact with those who knew Jesus and the apostles. Tradition for Irenaeus is organic, a living link with the age of the apostles. But it was not the only link.

The other link to the apostles, the other locus of authority, is Scripture, the Old Testament of course, but also the books of the New Testament, which he calls "scripture," *graphe*. The most important of these are the four gospels, which he lists in the order of Matthew, Mark, Luke, and John, the now traditional order. Significantly he includes

John, a favorite of the Gnostics and previously a questionable book to some catholic Christians (*A.H.* 3,1,1). He calls Mark Peter's disciple and interpreter, and Luke Paul's companion, recognizing that their gospels, although not by apostles, contain apostolic teaching. He argues that there can be only four gospels, no more or less, because there are four principal regions of the world, four principal winds, and four cherubim in the vision of John (Revelation 4). This seems specious to us, but in the Ancient World arguments from "natural" phenomena were important. Clement of Rome considers the phoenix, a bird which regenerates itself asexually every 500 years, to be a symbol of Christ's resurrection (ch. 25).

Irenaeus is the first Christian in history to use the Acts of the Apostles, and thus the first proof - outside the book itself - that Acts ever existed. He knows Revelation, 1 Peter, 1-2 John, and all the Pauline epistles, except Philemon. (It is understandable that he does not use it since that epistle offers little to the theologian.) Only once (*A.H.* 1,6,3) does he refer to the Pauline corpus as scriptural, but it is difficult to believe that an Asian who knew Polycarp would reject Paul.

Irenaeus occasionally includes words of Jesus not known from the New Testament (*A.H.* 2, 46, 1; 5,36,1), and his Christian *graphe* includes the second-century prophetic book the *Shepherd* of Hermas. Yet the main lines of the future canon are there: the four gospels, Acts, the Pauline corpus, some Catholic Epistles, and Revelation. Furthermore, they are there to be cited and used in theological debate just as the Old Testament could be cited and used. Finally, and most importantly for Irenaeus, the books were read in the Church. Unlike later writers, he did not set the Bible against the Church nor did he exalt either tradition or scripture above the other. "It behooves us, therefore, to avoid their (the Gnostics') doctrines, and to take careful heed lest we suffer injury from them; but to flee to the Church, and be brought up in her bosom, and to be nourished with the Lord's scripture." (*A.H.* 5,20,2).

Scripture and tradition are complementary. They are not two distinct sources of revelation but two modes of transmission which work harmoniously.

With Irenaeus the existence of a collection of authoritative Christian books is now a fact. The question was now, which books belonged in that collection? Although not until 367 did anyone suggest our twenty-seven, we must not think that in between there was nothing but confusion or that anyone who wished to make up a list could do so. Questions on the canon rarely dealt with the gospels, Acts, the Pauline corpus, 1 Peter or 1 John. Rather they were about Hebrews, Revelation, and the remaining Catholic epistles. They were also about books not now in the canon.

H. Which Books?

We will not trace a path through all the debates and all the lists but will just point out a few of the more prominent markers along the way. In general, the criteria for inclusion were apostolicity and orthodoxy. Apostolicity never meant mere antiquity; for example, the epistles of Clement of Rome and Ignatius were never serious candidates for the New Testament because their authors clearly considered themselves post-apostolic. Nor did it mean just works by Paul and members of the Twelve. To be sure, most of the books were thought to be by them, but apostolicity also meant harmony with apostolic teaching, and it extended to Mark and Luke who were definitely not apostles. Furthermore, several Fathers knew that Paul did not write Hebrews and that John the apostle did not write Revelation, but they did not consider this a reason to keep them from the canon. As for orthodoxy, it meant the current orthodoxy of the second and third centuries. Only Revelation encountered problems with this criterion because its apocalyptic imaginings were not taken seriously in the third century.

The Western canon lists begin with the Muratorian fragment, named for Ludovico Muratori who discovered it in 1740. The manuscript containing it is a Medieval one, but scholars date the text itself *circa* 200. This is a partial canon list, which in its entirety may have included both Old and New Testament books. The fragment starts with a half-sentence and then a reference to Luke as the third gospel, so presumably Matthew and Mark preceded Luke. The list includes the four gospels, followed by the "acts of all the apostles" of Luke, the Pauline epistles in the order of the seven communities and the three individuals to whom Paul wrote, that is, the Corinthians, Ephesians, Philippians, Colossians, Galatians, Thessalonians, and Romans, then Philemon, Titus, and Timothy. This division is important to the author because John wrote to seven churches in Revelation, and the author appreciates the parallel. Next come Jude and two unnumbered epistles of John, one of which is 1 John since the author alludes to it. He then lists the Wisdom of Solomon and the apocalypses of John and Peter, although he admits some have doubts about the latter. Wisdom is an odd inclusion, and no other early Christian list has it. 1 Peter is a surprising exclusion, and it may result from an error by the Medieval scribe who copied the text.

The author rejects the books of Marcion and some Gnostic sects, and he sets out a strong argument against inclusion of the apocalyptic *Shepherd* of Hermas, which implies it was accepted or at least a candidate for acceptance in his church. He claims the *Shepherd* was written when Pius, Hermas' brother, was bishop of Rome (*circa* 140-150) and the book was thus not apostolic. We cannot be sure of this document's influence, but the *Shepherd* appears in no Western canon lists later than this one.

Also *circa* 200 an obscure figure named Gaius of Rome claimed that a Gnostic heretic named Cerinthus wrote the Gospel of John and Revelation. His views are similar to some anti-Montanists in Asia Minor called Alogi because of their opposition to John's gospel (which speaks of the Logos, as does Revelation, the only two New Testament books to do so). Gaius' views, however, had little effect on the West, where those books were routinely accepted as apostolic. But his objections illustrate how controversial the canonicity question could become, since some Christians thought that books by known heretics were considered by others to be inspired by God.

The Roman presbyter Hippolytus (*ca.* 170-236), a pupil of Irenaeus, follows his teacher, except that he includes 2 Peter but not 2 John. Like Irenaeus, he does not cite Philemon, but this is almost certainly because of its brevity and irrelevance to most Christian teaching. The African Tertullian (*ca.* 160 - *ca.* 225) also follows Irenaeus, but he accepts Jude and does not include 2 John. The absentees from all these lists are 3 John, Hebrews, and James, and this situation in the West will remain so until the second half of the fourth century.

I. The Alexandrians

In the East the situation was different. Clement of Alexandria (*ca.* 150 - *ca.* 215) lived in a cosmopolitan, liberal environment. He was open to diverse influences, and he accepted many of them. He considered both the Old and New Testaments to be scripture. He accepted twenty-four new Testament books, all but James, 2 Peter, and 3 John; he did not actually mention Philemon but scholars again think the omission of no significance. Clement openly accepted Hebrews which he thought Paul wrote to the Jews in their own tongue but which Luke later translated into Greek, and that accounted for the difference in style. But Clement also considered the *Epistle of Barnabas* to be an inspired work of Paul's companion, and he considered 1 Clement, the *Shepherd* of Hermas, the *Preaching of Peter* and the *Apocalypse of Peter* to be inspired. He called the *Didache* scripture, and although he said the Church accepts four gospels, he quotes by name the *Gospel according to the Hebrews* and the *Gospel according to the Egyptians*. If this were not enough, he also cites sayings of Jesus from no known canonical or apocryphal source.

He further complicated all this by his incessant mixture of biblical and classical quotations. He quotes non-Christian authors twice as often as Christian authors. He simply did not consider the Bible as the only authority. In his work *Stromateis* (I,5 [28,1]) he wrote:

> Philosophy was necessary to the Greeks for righteousness, until the coming of the Lord; and even now it is useful for the development of true religion, as a kind of preparatory discipline for those who arrive at faith by way of demonstration.... For God is the source of all good; either directly, as in the Old and New Testaments, or indirectly, as in the case of philosophy. But it may even be that philosophy was given to the Greeks directly; for it was a schoolmaster, to bring Hellenism to Christ, as the Law was for the Hebrews.

A native of Greece and a converted pagan, he saw God behind the great achievements of the pagans, and he did not shrink from putting philosophy, that is, secular learning, on a par with the Old Testament as a preparatory to Christianity for the Gentiles. Clement does not advance the notion of the canon very much, but he does demonstrate what an involved process it was for the Church to arrive at the New Testament we take for granted.

Clement does, however, deserve a place in the history of the canon because he was the first person unambiguously to use the phrase "New Testament" for his collection of Christian scriptures. He did it frequently, as in the passage just cited. The name did not catch on immediately, and his younger contemporary Origen can refer to "the so-called New Testament," but the name and the books have finally been linked.

The greatest biblical scholar of Christian Antiquity was another Alexandrian, Origen (*ca.* 185-254). He considered himself very much the churchman, and his views on the canon probably represent those of the Alexandrian church. *Circa* 230, after a dispute with Bishop Demetrias, Origen left Alexandria for Caesarea in Palestine where he found different views on the canon, and he moderated his own views.

Origen acknowledges various kinds of New Testament

books. There are those to be accepted, those in doubt, and those to be rejected. In the first category are the four gospels, Acts, fourteen Pauline epistles (including Hebrews and Philemon which he specifically mentions), James, Jude, 1 Peter, 1 John, and Revelation. He knows Paul did not write Hebrews but the epistle showed Pauline influence. The remaining three books in our canon, 2 Peter, 2-3 John, are in the disputed category. While at Alexandria he accepted *Barnabas*, the *Shepherd* of Hermas, and the *Didache*, but in Caesarea he showed more reserve about them. His views on 1 Clement are uncertain. He condemns several Gnostic gospels. It is important that the twenty-four books he did accept are all in the canon today.

Between 253 and 257 an incident occurred which shows how the notion of the canon had developed. When some Egyptian visionaries showed excessive and even troublesome apocalyptic tendencies and appealed for support to the Revelation of John, which they interpreted literally, Dionysius, bishop of Alexandria (247 - *ca*. 264), replied by showing that the book should be understood figuratively. In the course of his discussion of the book, he wrote an impressive stylistic analysis of Revelation and John's gospel. He proved that the author of the gospel, by now universally accepted as John of the Twelve, could not have written Revelation (Eusebius, *H.E.* 7, 24-25). He points out that some people would reject the book, that is, keep it from the canon, but he himself would not dare to reject it, even though he could prove it was not the work of an apostle, because he thinks it inspired and many Christians have a high opinion of it, that is, it is accepted in the Church. The use of a New Testament book by the community had given it an authority independent of its supposed apostolic authorship. Apostolicity without authorship by an apostle or a known disciple of an apostle - the fruits of Irenaeus' work can clearly be seen.

Dionysius' support was decisive for Alexandria, but Revelation continued to be questioned in other parts of the Greek East. In Syria, for example, Lucian of Antioch (d. *ca*.

312) rejected it, and Amphilochius of Iconium (*ca.* 340-395) says it was widely repudiated.

J. The Closing of the Canon

The church historian Eusebius of Caesarea (*ca.* 260 - *ca.* 340), who has preserved so many other statements about the canon, himself shows the New Testament canon in its second-last stage. There are the accepted books: the four gospels, Acts, the fourteen Pauline epistles (including Hebrews), 1 Peter, 1 John, and Revelation, although Eusebius admits there are doubts about the last. Next are five 'disputed books': James, Jude, 2 Peter, 2-3 John, that is, the rest of the twenty-seven. All the other worthwhile books, such as *Barnabas* and the *Shepherd*, are "spurious." Heretical writings, such as the *Gospel of Thomas*, are to be completely rejected (*H.E.* 3.25).

In 367, Athanasius, bishop of Alexandria (*ca.* 296-373; bishop from 328), takes the final step. In a condemnation of heretical attempts to introduce apocryphal works into the Scriptures, he lists the Alexandrian canon of the Old and New Testaments. For the first time the twenty-seven books accepted today are specifically listed as the books of the New Testament, although not in the familiar order. The Catholic Epistles precede the Pauline ones, and Hebrews stands between 2 Thessalonians and 1 Timothy.

This did not completely settle the question. Cyril of Jerusalem (d. 368) did not accept Revelation, and John Chrysostom (d. 408) never mentioned it, but by the mid-fifth century the Greek-speaking Easterners accepted all the books first listed by Athanasius. In Syriac-speaking areas, Revelation continued to be omitted from the canon, often with 2 Peter, 2-3 John, and Jude. The final acceptance of a twenty-seven book canon among all the Eastern churches had to wait for the Middle Ages.

Doctrinal controversies in the fourth century brought East and West into frequent contact, and Eastern notions on the canon tilted the balance in the West. Hilary of Poitiers (d. 367) and Lucifer of Cagliari (d. 370) accepted Hebrews, and in 393 official sanction for our twenty-seven books came at a council at Hippo Regius in Africa. Two more African councils, meeting in Carthage in 397 and 419, reaffirmed this decision. The immense prestige of St. Augustine stood behind the African canon, and he listed the twenty-seven New Testament books in his *De Doctrina Christiana* (2,8). By 405 the papacy accepted this canon, and there is disputed evidence that this could have happened as early as 382.

The canon remained settled until the Renaissance when humanist scholars raised questions about the authorship of certain books. Cardinal Cajetan doubted whether Hebrews, James, Jude, and 2-3 John were actually written by their supposed authors, and he considered them to have less authority. Martin Luther interpreted the New Testament largely in terms of his interpretation of Paul, and he wished to excise James and Revelation from the canon. But more moderate views prevailed among both Catholics and Protestants, and all Western denominations have kept a New Testament of twenty-seven equally authoritative books.

5

THE NEW TESTAMENT
APOCRYPHAL BOOKS

The terms New Testament Apocrypha, or Apocryphal New Testament refer to those writings which claim to be by or about New Testament figures, but which are not in the canon. The terms are vague because there is no way to put a limit on such writings, although editors of the apocrypha such as Edgar Hennecke, Wilhelm Schneelmelcher, and Montague Rhodes James usually do not include texts written later than the fifth or sixth century, and most of the apocrypha in their editions are of the fourth century or earlier. In the fourth and fifth centuries, when the New Testament canon was finally being closed, churchmen commonly condemned the reading of apocryphal literature, although without much effect. Modern scholars take a tolerant and even positive view of this literature, for example, the great French patristic scholar Jean Danielou, S.J., who proved the value of the apocrypha for understanding early Jewish Christianity, usually considered a poor relation to the Greek and Latin varieties. It is now taken for granted that the apocrypha can tell us a great deal about Christian life and thought, especially among groups like the Gnostics.

Like the canon, the apocrypha demand that we reconsider our presuppositions. Because we consider the twenty-seven canonical books as the only divinely inspired books of Early Christianity, we often treat them as if they were hermetically sealed off from the rest of the Early Christian literature, especially from the apocryphal books which were candidates for the canon and from which the canon had to be protected. But if we take this view, we will misunderstand not only the apocrypha but also the New Testament, which in some ways differed very little from the apocrypha.

Some parts of the apocryphal *Gospel of Thomas* probably date as early as the first century, while others are definitely of the early second century, so, as with the earliest Fathers, the apocrypha cannot be separated from the New Testament on the basis of chronological priority.

The apocrypha of the early second century were composed when there was still no canon, so their authors, like the scriptural authors, did not write them as candidates for a canon. They wrote their books for a variety of reasons but not to pervert a non-existent New Testament.

Many apocryphal writings claim to be by members of the Twelve or by Paul, such as the *Apocalypse of Peter* or the *Vision of Paul*. At first sight this could seem like a devious device for getting canonical status and apostolic authority for these books. But as we saw in chapter three, Matthew of the Twelve did not write Matthew's gospel, nor did Peter write 2 Peter, nor did Paul write the Pastorals, nor did John of the Twelve write Revelation. Furthermore, most scholars would deny apostolic authority to James, Jude, 1 Peter, the Johannine gospel and epistles, while a sizeable number reject Pauline authorship of Ephesians, and some others doubt the authenticity of Colossians and 2 Thessalonians. We Christians can hardly accuse the ancient apocryphal writers of using pseudonyms as a device to ferret their books into the "apostolic" canon. Indeed, if canonicity requires that the books be written by those to whom they are attributed, our modern New Testament would not be much larger than Marcion's.

Finally, some scholars think that the *Gospel of Thomas* contains or at least reflects some authentic sayings of Jesus. (Recall that many Christian writers, Clement of Rome,

Irenaeus, Justin Martyr, Clement of Alexandria, preserved non-canonical sayings of the Lord.) Since we know that some sayings attributed to Jesus in the canonical writings were insights of the early Church and were put into Jesus' mouth by the evangelists, there is a real possibility that authentic sayings of Jesus survive in non-canonical works, while non-authentic sayings survive in canonical works. To be sure, canonicity does not require authenticity, but this does show that a strict dichotomy between canonical and apocryphal can be very misleading.

Basically there are three kinds of apocryphal works. First, there are those written in much the same way as the canonical books, that is, a particular community of individuals wished to express a certain viewpoint, probably in response to a current need. This written expression was later thought by some to be as authoritative as the newly canonical books, but in the course of time the Catholic Church decided that this was not the case. These books could have come from any community, orthodox or heterodox. Second, there are those which were deliberately written as partisan documents to advance a particular idea, cause, or person, and they were given New Testament attributes to gain authority. The so-called "Correspondence between Jesus and Abgar" falls into this category. Third, there are the documents which can best be described as a combination of piety and curiosity, and whose authors never intended them to have canonical status. These documents, usually with lively and picturesque accounts of the lives of Jesus and his disciples, were often enormously popular, and they influenced preachers, story-tellers, and artists. For example, the famous frescoes by the Italian painter Giotto in the Scrovegni Chapel in Padua, Italy, depict the parents of Mary, Joachim and Anna, neither of whom are mentioned in the canonical gospels but who first appear in the Protoevangelium of James, a second-century apocryphon. (It is, of course, possible that Mary's parents were named Joachim and Anna, but the key point is the popularity among Christians of non-canonical materials.) Inevitably there was much overlapping between these various types of apocryphal literature, for example, an imaginative or pious narrative of Peter's or Paul's adventures could contain the theological views of a particular community.

People accustomed to a closed canon may find it strange that good, even pious Christians could make up accounts of Jesus and the apostles, but if we think about it, we realize that it is actually very natural, and we even do it today. By the early second century, everyone who had known Jesus in the flesh was dead, and even those who had known the apostles were passing into history. Christians knew the Lord and his disciples only through the New Testament, which really does not tell us very much. For example, the synoptic gospels, apart from the infancy narratives and Luke's story of Jesus in the Temple, recount less than one year of Jesus's life. It was natural to wonder what else Jesus had done, especially as child or young adult before his public career. It is just as natural for us, dependent upon written sources, to wonder what impression he made on the people who actually met him in the flesh. They were, after all, people like us. How did he affect their lives? And what about the apostles whose stories are not recounted in Acts? And what did Peter and Paul do after they arrived in Rome?

Throughout history Christians have been filling in the details, and the scripturally sophisticated twentieth-century has continued the tradition. We may distinguish canonical from non-canonical, but that does not prevent us from enjoying the non-canonical. When we prepare nativity scenes at Christmas, we routinely include an ox and an ass even though the infancy narratives do not mention them. We include three kings even though Matthew mentions not kings but only magi, and he does not give their number. (He mentions three gifts - Matt 2:11). In the traditional hymn "We Three Kings" we sing that Jesus was "born a king on Bethlehem's plain," when, in fact, Bethelehem is on a hill, while a modern American carol has a little drummer boy going to see the infant Jesus and playing his drum for him. The best-selling novels of Taylor Caldwell, *Dear and Glorious Physician* and *Great Lion of God*, imaginatively recreate the early lives of Luke and Paul, and mass-market films like "The Robe" and "Ben-Hur" deal with people whose lives were changed by contact with Jesus. These "neo-apocrypha" are not limited just to popular culture. In music, Gian-Carlo Menotti's opera "Amahl and the Night Visitors" tells of a crippled boy who is healed when the magi stop in his home on their way to Bethlehem. In literature, the great British author Graham Greene wrote the short story "The Second Death" about the final death of the widow's son whom Jesus resurrected (Luke 7:11-17), and his fictional narrator is the blind man whom Jesus cured by placing a clay made from spittle on his eyes (John 9:1-7). Like all the other early Christians, the composers and readers of the apocrypha were not very different from us.

The New Testament apocrypha are extensive. The collections of Hennecke-Schneelmelcher and James as well as the Gnostic collection of James Robinson combine for more than 2,000 pages, and even they do not include everything. (There is, of course, considerable overlapping in these editions.) Here we will simply outline the types of literature and look at some of the more important books.

A. Gospels

The apocrypha contain the same types of literature as the canonical scriptures, that is, gospels, acts, epistles, and apocalypses. Although the epistle was the most popular literary form in the New Testament and among the early Fathers, the other forms predominate in the apocrypha. Gospels are naturally the most popular because they told of Jesus, and groups claiming the Lord's authority were anxious to have documents showing him as the source of their teaching. The gospel attributions range widely, from apostles like Peter, Thomas, and Philip, to religious groups like the Nazareans and Ebionites, to individual Christians like Mary Magdalene and Nicodemus, to heresiarchs like Basilides and Mani.

The most important gospel is probably that of Thomas, a Gnostic work from Syria or Egypt, which dates *circa* 140. It differs from traditional gospels, consisting of a collection of

114 sayings, or *logia*, of Jesus, many of which parallel the canonical gospels and some of which may go back to authentic first-century traditions. The gospel presents Thomas as the guardian of the secret sayings of Jesus, and the book was probably intended for a limited number of readers. A collection of logia proves the author and his community were more interested in Jesus' teaching than in his life, possibly because his life involved him in the world of matter. In common Gnostic fashion, the work emphasizes the importance of knowledge for personal salvation, and it often downplays the physical.

The Gnostic gospel of Philip is also of the second century and from Egypt. It, too, is a collection, but a melange of sayings, observations, and ethical injunctions. It speaks highly of marriage, suggests that the division of man and woman at the dawn of history caused all the trouble in the world, and emphasizes the female element in religion - the Holy Spirit is female and the three "who always walked with the Lord" are all named Mary.

The Apocryphon of John is yet another second-century Gnostic work from Egypt, but it deals largely with the creation of the world as revealed to John, son of Zebedee. This heavily mythological account tells of the struggle between light and darkness, a favorite theme in the canonical John. Jesus comes from heaven to remind us of our heavenly origin. Those who will possess the knowledge he gives can return to their home, the realm of light, while everyone else faces constant reincarnation. Its negative view of matter led the Gnostic sect which produced this gospel to stress asceticism.

The Gospel of Mary is a third-century Gnostic document which survives in fragmentary form from Egypt. The Mary of the title is Mary Magdalene, a favorite of the Gnostics because according to a canonical gospel she had spoken to the Risen Lord with no one else around (John 20:11-18), and so they could claim her as a source for otherwise unknown traditions. In this brief text, Mary tells the apostles of her vision of Jesus and gives an account of the soul's struggles against evils. Andrew merely disagrees with her, but Peter disparages the very idea that Jesus spoke to a woman in preference to the male apostles. Levi tells Peter that he is always hot-headed, and if Jesus made Mary worthy, why should the apostles reject her? (This could be a play on Jesus' words to Peter in Acts 10:15.)

A church Father named Epiphanius of Salamis (*ca.* 315-403) reports on a Gnostic gospel called "The Questions of Mary" which told of an apparition to her by Jesus who justified sexual activities outside marriage. Many Christian sects dichotomized body and spirit, and favored the spirit. Some, like those who produced the Apocryphon of John, favored disciplining the body by asceticism and abstinence from sex, while others reasoned that since bodies do not really count for anything, they could do what they wanted with them and that sexual license was permissible. Here one group like that has blatantly attributed its own ideas to Jesus via Mary Magdalen.

Over the centuries the Infancy Gospels have proven most popular, especially the Protoevangelium of James and the Infancy Gospel of Thomas. "James" tells of the miraculous birth of Mary to Joachim and Anna, her consecration as a virgin in the Temple, the Temple priests' concern to marry her off when she polluted the holy place by her puberty, the miraculous choice of Joseph to be her husband, the angelic annunciation and the birth of Jesus, Herod's search for Jesus and John the Baptist, and Herod's murder of John's father Zacharias. The "proto-evangelium" or "earliest good news" (because it begins with the birth of Mary) dates to the mid-second century and could be from Syria or Egypt. It is the first evidence of Mariology, that is, a concern with Mary's place in the economy of salvation. It glorifies her, and through her it glorifies virginity, and that guaranteed it a warm reception in the East. It was condemned in Gaul (modern France) or Italy in the fifth century, but happily for Christian art and literature this condemnation never affected its popularity.

The other infancy gospel, that of Thomas, deals with the childhood of Jesus. It contains famous stories such as his making living pigeons out of clay models, but in general this gospel presents him as a detestable little brat who shows off his miraculous powers and often uses them vindictively. Jesus withers the arm of a man who disturbs his game, strikes dead a child who runs by and accidentally bumps into him, and inflicts blindness on bystanders who criticize him for killing the child. This strange but fascinating gospel shows the transferral of primitive folklore motifs into Christian literature. Not surprisingly, this was never a candidate for the canon in spite of its second century date. It may have originated in Syria.

Most gospels tell of Jesus' life, but the Gospel of Nicodemus tells what Jesus did between his death and resurrection. This gospel also includes the Acts of Pilate, a brief account of what Pilate did after the crucifixion. It dates to the fourth century, and it originated in the Greek East but where is uncertain. The gospel opens with Jesus' trial before Pilate, who is very sympathetically portrayed. The Roman sincerely tries to get Jesus released, but at last he gives in to the mob and orders Jesus to be crucified with two criminals, Gestas and Dysmas (the good thief). The second portion of the gospel tells of Jesus' liberation of all the good people who died before his coming, from Adam and Seth through David and Elijah to his contemporaries John the Baptist and Lazarus. Jesus, the King of Glory, easily vanquishes Satan and Hades (Death) by smashing Hell's brass doors and iron bars. Since the canonical scriptures say almost nothing about Jesus in the realm of the dead (cf. 1 Peter 3:19), there were unlimited possibilities for the imagination, and this anonymous author used them.

This book's popularity was manifested in many ways. By the sixth century an anonymous translator brought out a Latin version, and that in turn spawned vernacular Western versions, including the famous English Medieval play cycle *The Harrowing of Hell.* As for the Pilate stories, some Christians so furthered the process of exonerating him for guilt in Jesus' death that among the Coptic Christians of Egypt he is venerated as a saint.

Imagination plus ecclesiastical politics produced the correspondence of Christ with Abgar V, toparch of Edessa

(9-46 A.D.). Eusebius of Caesarea records the story (*H.E.* 1.13). Abgar hears of Jesus and his wondrous deeds and also of Jewish hostility toward him, so he offers him refuge in Edessa. Jesus replies that Abgar is blessed to have believed without seeing, but that he (Jesus) must remain in Judea and fulfill what he was sent to do. After the Ascension, Jesus' disciple Thaddeus goes to Edessa to evangelize, and while there he cures Abgar of a disease. The legend was probably created by the orthodox party in Edessa to strengthen their hand against the Marcionites by stressing the apostolicity of their church. Eusebius obligingly incorporated it into his history, thus giving it an aura of authenticity as well as considerable prestige. This forgery was never considered canonical.

B. Epistles

The epistles are fewer and generally less interesting, but two are worth mentioning. Colossians 4:16 speaks of an epistle of Paul to Laodicea, which encouraged someone in the West between the second and fourth centuries to write in Latin an epistle to the Laodiceans. It is a pastiche of Pauline phrases, largely from Philippians, but it managed to secure a place in several important Medieval Latin manuscripts of the New Testament. Why anyone created this forgery no one knows. Possibly some enthusiast for Paul envisioned himself as aiding the apostle's reputation by filling in a gap in the Pauline collection.

Another Latin-speaking enthusiast for Paul composed an exchange of letters between Paul and Seneca, the tutor of Nero and, like Paul, a victim of the emperor's wrath. (Seneca was forced by Nero to commit suicide.) This correspondence, composed in Italy in the third century, was accepted as authentic by the Church Father Jerome in the fourth century, although by that time inclusion in the canon was out of the question. The letters deal with Seneca's interest in Christianity and his hopes for its success in Rome. They make good reading, and even today it is exciting to think of possible contacts between the greatest Christian writer and the greatest pagan philosopher of the first century.

C. Acts

The apocryphal acts are generally the longest works. They provided room for narrative imagination because the careers of the apostles were or could have been so much longer than Jesus'. There are acts for several apostles, including John, Andrew, Matthew, and Paul's companion Barnabas, but the three most famous and influential are those of Peter, Paul, and Thomas.

It is the unanimous tradition of the Early Church that Peter went to Rome, a tradition which the New Testament supports. "Peter" writes from "Babylon" (1 Peter 5:13), a Christian code name for Rome (Revelation 17:5,9). But what did Peter do in Rome? The historical traditions are minimal, but the Acts of Peter fills in the details. The story centers around the conflict between Peter and Simon Magus, who appears as a magician in Acts 8:9-24. The climax of the conflict comes when Simon amazes the Romans by flying. This demoralizes the Christians who turn to Peter for help. He prays to God that Simon will fall from the sky, but not be killed. Simons falls and is crippled, and the Romans then abandon him, follow Peter, and believe in Christ. This narrative shows the glorious triumph of the faith, but the author then has to explain Nero's persecution of the Christians. He blames it on the sexual desires of the Roman, pagan men.

The writer of the Acts of Peter enthusiastically champions sexual abstinence, and not just for unmarried people. When Peter converts Roman women to Christianity, they cease having relations with their husbands; the concubines of noble Romans do likewise. With much understatement the author says (ch. 34), "So there was the greatest disquiet in Rome." The angry pagan men plot against Peter, who, reluctantly and only under pressure from other Christians, agrees to leave Rome. The Christians who stay behind face their wrath, that is, a persecution.

This semi-comic passage provides an incongruous introduction to the most beautiful section of the story. As Peter leaves Rome and certain death, he has a vision of Jesus going toward the city. Peter asks him, "Lord, where are you going?," which in Latin reads *Domine, quo vadis*? Jesus replies that he goes to Rome to be crucified again. Peter awakes from the vision, understands the divine message, and returns to Rome where he is crucified. The Gospel of John refers to a martyr's death for Peter (21:18-19), but the Acts of Peter first tells the famous story of his being crucified upside down. The original text of this work was composed in Greek *circa* 180 and either in Rome or Asia Minor. It provides the basis for two novels, *Quo Vadis* by the Polish author Henryk Sienkiewicz and *The Silver Chalice* by Thomas Costain.

The Acts of Paul is unique in one regard: we know something about its composition. The African author Tertullian, writing *circa* 200, says in his book *On Baptism* (ch. 17), "If those who read the writings that wrongly carry the name of Paul bring forth the example of Thecla in order to defend the right of women to baptize, they should know that the presbyter in Asia (Minor) who wrote this document, as if he himself could further Paul's prestige, was removed from office after he had been convicted and admitted he had done it from love of Paul." Tertullian alludes to the other leading character in the story, Thecla, whose Acts are occasionally preserved separately from the larger work, but since her acts would not have furthered Paul's prestige, Tertullian knew of the whole work. The presbyter from Asia is anonymous, and he was not removed from office so much for heresy as for presumption. Tertullian thought any account which spoke of women baptizing to be heretical, but the Acts of Paul appears to be an orthodox work, and it probably was indeed written out of love.

The author has set the story in Asia Minor, the site of much of Paul's missionary work. In the town of Iconium

Paul converts a virgin named Thecla, who decides to abandon her engagement and become a perpetual virgin. Her enraged fiance stirs up the populace against Paul and Thecla, who are condemned to death. As Thecla is in the arena with the beasts, she sees a large pit of water. Being unbaptized, she plunges into the pit to baptize herself. She survives the beasts and later becomes a missionary.

Paul also got away from Iconium, only to be condemned to the beasts at Ephesus, where a ferocious lion rushes at him, but instead of devouring him, it lies down at his feet. It turns out that Paul had encountered the lion in an earlier part of the story, and he had even baptized it! After this Paul went to Philippi where he wrote his Third Letter to the Corinthians, a melange of citations from genuine Pauline epistles and the Pastorals. The story ends with Paul in Rome where Nero, fearful of the kingship of Jesus, persecutes the Christians. In this persecution Paul is decapitated.

Many elements in this story, such as the baptized lion which refuses to harm Paul, are obvious folklore motifs, but some others might be biographically accurate. For example, as a Roman citizen Paul could not be crucified but merited the quicker death of decapitation, so the report of his death fits the historical situation. Wilhelm Schneelmelcher, an editor of New Testament apocrypha, and other scholars think the description of Paul given in chapter 3, a standard mode in Christian art for centuries, may be based on Paul's actual appearance: "... a man of small stature, with a bald head and crooked legs in a good state of body, with eyebrows meeting and a nose somewhat hooked..." This description does not contradict 2 Corinthians 10:10: "His bodily presence is weak." On the other hand, the American scholar Robert Grant has argued persuasively that the author borrowed the description from one given of a prominent pagan in another ancient work.

[This description of Paul may not make him sound like a cinematic leading man, but he sounds a lot better looking than Jesus. In general Early Christian writers, such as Justin Martyr, Irenaeus, Tertullian, Clement of Alexandria, and Origen, thought that Jesus was ugly. They based this on

Isaiah 53:2: "... he had no comeliness that we should look at him, and no beauty that we should desire him." A few authors thought he might have been good-looking, while a few others with some docetic leanings thought he could adapt his appearance to the viewer.

The Acts of Paul also tells us that Barsabas Justus (Acts 2:23) had flat feet. Maybe that is why he did not get into the Twelve?]

The most important work of this kind is the Acts of Thomas, written in the third century, possibly in Edessa since scholars think its original language was Syriac. It tells of Thomas' missionary endeavors in India, and although no one incident in the book can be singled out as historical, the book might reflect a genuine historical situation when Christian missionaries went to India in the second or even the first century. The closing verses of Matthew's gospel (28:19-20) portray Jesus urging the eleven disciples to "Go therefore and make disciples of all nations," so the idea of missionary work beyond the Roman pale was in the first-century Christian consciousness. Acts 8:26-40 recounts the baptism of an Ethiopian eunuch who was returning home, so Luke gives a small but symbolic example of the faith going past the Roman frontiers. There were regular commercial sea voyages between the Roman Empire and India as well as overland caravans, so the missionaries certainly could have reached it. Eusebius (*H.E.* 5, 10, 2) says that Pantaenus, the Sicilian who founded the catechetical school in Alexandria, evangelized in India in the second century. There were definitely Christians in India in the fourth century, and the Indian Christians have traditionally regarded Thomas as the founder of their church, although they could have adopted this tradition from the Acts of Thomas. Whether or not the Acts have an historical basis, India provides an exotic setting for what is a romantic novel with long didactic sections and two hymns, including the famous "Hymn of the Pearl" (9th. Act, chs. 108-113).

The story follows much the same pattern as the Acts of Peter. Thomas goes to India, performs miracles, proclaims, and eventually converts the king, Gundophorus. The apostle then goes on to the adjacent territory of King Misdaeus. He converts a noblewoman named Mygdonia who then ceases to have sexual relations with her husband Charisius, who persecutes Thomas and eventually has him martyred by being pierced with spears. A Christian convert reverently carries Thomas' bones to the West.

At one point in the story, while he is in prison, Thomas chants the "Hymn of the Pearl," a precious jewel which the son of "the King of Kings" (who probably represents God the Father) must travel to Egypt to fetch away from a guardian serpent. When the son takes the pearl, he sheds the "dirty and unclean" garment which the people of Egypt had given him. The pearl represents the soul and the garment the body. The son returns safely with the pearl. The Gnostic tendencies are mild, although this might be due to later orthodox editing of a very popular story.

D. Apocalypses

Apocalyptic was a Jewish literary genre which had a limited appeal in Gentile circles. Outside the canonical Apocalypse and the *Shepherd* of Hermas, the most important Christian apocalypses are those of Peter and Paul. Ironically, these apocalypses are not very apocalyptic. They do not deal with Christ's coming in glory but with the fates of individuals in the next life.

The Apocalypse of Peter is quite early, most likely dating to the early or mid-second century. The Muratorian Fragment and other lists show that for a while it was a candidate for the canon. Possibly it was written in Egypt. Its popularity and use were considerable. In the early fourth century, Methodius of Olympus (d. *ca.* 311) still considered it inspired.

The book tells how Jesus grants to Peter visions of heaven and hell. Not surprisingly the vision of hell offers more dramatic scenes, for example, naked women hanged by their hair and then dropped into a fiery pit, and men buried upside down in mire. Loathsome vermin and other animals abound, and they join in the torture of the damned. By contrast, heaven is a great garden filled with fair trees and blessed fruits, reminiscent of Eden. The author exercises his fertile imagination, and his teaching is basically moral, if weighed a bit toward sternness. The work has no heterodox tendencies, and this probably enhanced its appeal.

Unlike the Apocalypse of Peter, the Apocalypse of Paul was never a candidate for the canon because of its late date, the second half of the fourth century. It was originally composed in Greek, but under the title *Visio Pauli*, the Latin version was enormously popular in the West in the Early Middle Ages. The anonymous author takes advantage of Paul's statement in 2 Corinthians 12:1-10 that he had been caught up to the third heaven where he "heard things that cannot be told" (v. 4). The author of this apocalypse tells them.

The book begins with an anonymous Christian living in Tarsus in 388. An angel tells him to dig up the foundation of his house. When he does, he discovers the Apocalypse of Paul encased in the marble box. The apocalypse tells of Paul's rapture to the third heaven where he sees angels giving daily reports on the deeds of humans. Paul then sails on a golden ship to heaven where he sees many Old Testament figures. After that he visits hell where the damned include bishops, presbyters, deacons, and lectors, a rather barbed comment on the Imperial Christianity of the fourth century. Paul then returns to heaven. After that point, the text breaks off.

E. The Apocrypha and the Canon

This brief account has shown the range of the apocryphal works, and, I hope, stimulated some interest in them. Some are entertaining, others verbose and boring, all tell us about the Christians who produced them, and a few may even contain kernels of history.

The apocryphal works also tell us about the canon. For example, there are a series of tales, probably from third-century Syria, called the "Pseudo-Clementine Recognitions" which recount the adventures of Clement of Rome, whose family becomes separated, but after a series of adventures, his mother, father, brothers, and he are reunited when they recognize - hence the title - each other in spite of changes in age and fortune. The delightfully silly stories teach a mild Gnosticism and a rather strict asceticism, but they also witness to the importance of Clement for some Christians since he merits his own acts and is associated with Peter.

In the provocative book *The Gnostic Gospels*, Elaine Pagels makes a much wider use of the apocrypha. She argues that scholars have traditionally adopted the view of the "orthodox" party, for example, Irenaeus, and thus they have been too hard on the Gnostics. She suggests that many Gnostic apocrypha were excluded from the canon because they challenged the power of the orthodox hierarchy. For example, orthodox bishops could view the Gnostic claim to a direct knowledge of God as a threat to their role as sacramental conduits to God and thus as a threat to their control of the Church. They might also see the Gnostic view of Christ's passion as a non-historical event as a weakening of the idea of martyrdom as an imitation of Christ and thus as a weakening of hierarchical power in organizing the Church against the threat of persecution. Even the outline in this chapter shows the prominent role women played in the Gnostic apocrypha as bearers of revelation; Pagels suggests that such a role for women was simply unacceptable to the male, orthodox hierarchy, and thus the Gnostic apocrypha could not find a place in the canon. She interprets the material almost completely in terms of ecclesiastical politics, and she pays insufficient attention to Christians as standing in the Old Testament and Jewish traditions toward orthodoxy, canonicity, and women, but she raises some intriguing questions and demonstrates the historical potential of the apocrypha.

In many ways the study of the New Testament apocrypha

is just beginning. It promises to tell us more and more about the Early Christians and the diverse forces and movements which gave us the New Testament. Like the canonical books, the apocrypha emerged from the lives of the earliest communities.

6

WHAT THE NEW TESTAMENT SAYS

In our earlier chapters we saw that our first Christian ancestors determined what books would be in the New Testament. In this chapter we will see how the Early Church determined what the New Testament says.

At first sight this seems like a puzzling comment. After all, the New Testament says what it says, and that is that. But, as usual, things are not simple as they seem. For example, many of us know at least parts of the New Testament, such as the Lord's Prayer or the Eight Beatitudes as well as many lesser known passages such as "Render unto Caesar that which is Caesar's." But if we think about it for a second, we realize that what we know is actually an English translation, and usually one which we learned as children, such as the Revised Standard Version or the Douay-Rheims version. But if we turn to the newer translations, we realize how many forms "what the New Testament said" can really take. The RSV and the Douay-Rheims version translate Matthew 6:9 with the familiar "Our Father, who art in heaven, hallowed be thy name." The Jerusalem Bible has "Our Father in heaven may your name be holy." The Good News for Modern Man says "Our Father in heaven, may your holy name be honored." The New American Bible reads "Our Father in heaven, hallowed be your name." All are close, but all are different. No translation can be considered to contain the exact words of Scripture. [This rather obvious point is often missed by extremely conservative evangelicals who consider the King James Version - ironically enough, prepared by a committee of Anglicans who would have had little sympathy for the evangelical approach to Christianity - to be the equivalent of the original text.]

This is not to say that one cannot rely upon a translation for the understanding of Scripture; on the contrary, the standard of translation today is very high and is a large element in the popularity of Bible-reading, especially among Roman Catholics. My point is simply that when we speak of what the New Testament says, we must realize that Jesus and other early Christians simply did not speak English, not even Elizabethan English.

Let us then assume that we can read Greek, the language of Paul, the evangelists, and all the other New Testament writers. We could consult one of the several Greek editions, and then we would know what the New Testament said. But our experience with the translations has made us cautious. How do we know that these editions are accurate, that they faithfully reproduce the Greek text of the writers.

We start by asking how we know that any edition of a book is accurate. In the case of a modern book, we assume that the author sent the publisher his or her typed or processed text, and the publisher saw that it was printed correctly. [Occasionally in books we see the Latin word *corrigenda*, that is, things to be corrected, followed by a list of errors and corrections.] But suppose we are reading a modern edition of an older work, like the novel *Middlemarch* by the nineteenth-century writer George Eliot; how then can accuracy be achieved? In this case we expect that the modern editor has consulted the first edition of the books and perhaps even the author's notes to guarantee that the modern edition is a faithful reproduction of the Victorian one. These are standard techniques used by any reputable publishing house, and we can generally be confident that we are reading what the author actually wrote.

But now let us jump back in history, to the ages before printing when all books were manuscripts, that is, they were written by hand (from the Latin *manuscriptum*, "written" - *scriptum*, "by hand" - *manu*). How can we be sure that an edition of something like the Magna Carta is correct. Here the editor's task is to look at the original manuscript written by the work's author (this manuscript is called the autograph), decipher the Medieval or ancient handwriting, and then get an accurate rendering.

This method, of course, is the way in which we would expect an editor of the New Testament to work, that is, to consult the autographs of the Gospels or to look at Paul's epistles as written by him or the disciples who wrote for him. (In 1 Thes 3:17, Paul says he is writing the greeting in his own hand, implying that someone else had written out the texts of the epistle.) But here is the major difficulty. *There is no autograph for any New Testament book* (nor are there any for the Old Testament books either). There is simply no way anyone can guarantee the accuracy of a Greek version of Romans, for example, by consulting the very letter Paul sent to the Roman community. In every case scholars must consult copies of those books made by other people. Furthermore, the copies that survive today were not made by one of the apostles' disciples or by a member of the communities for which the books were written, but by people who lived decades and usually centuries after the letter was written. No manuscript of a New Testament book survives from the first century, and from the second century there are only fragments. The oldest known portion of a New Testament book is a fragment (only 3.5 by 2.3 inches) of John's gospel, discovered in Egypt and dated by scholars *circa* 125. It contains five verses of the gospel, 18:31-33 on one side and 18:37-38 on the reverse. No scholar has claimed that even this oldest fragment is from John's autograph; it too is a copy. The earliest complete book would be one of several Pauline Epistles preserved in a manuscript dated *circa* 200.

The earliest complete New Testament dates to the fourth century.

This may sound problematic, but since we know that there are editions of the Greek New Testament, which people have been studying, commenting upon, translating, and preaching from for centuries, we realize that scholars have devised a method to produce a reliable edition, even without the autographs. This very complicated science is known as textual criticism, and we will devote the rest of this chapter to understanding how it works.

Before we do that, however, two points need to be made. The first concerns textual criticism. It is a very involved and complicated process; often its disputed points center on which manuscript of the New Testament or of a particular book should be consulted or preferred. In general, this chapter will not discuss any particular manuscript; the books by Jack Finegan and Bruce Metzger listed in the bibliography do that very well and at some length. Rather we will concentrate on how textual criticism works.

Second, we should explain why a chapter on textual criticism belongs in a book like this, which has emphasized the relation of Scripture to the community. After all, only a very small portion of the early Christians would have had anything to do with the copying and editing of the biblical books. There are two reasons why we are discussing textual criticism. The first is that a book on the making of the New Testament cannot leave out a description of how the very words of the biblical books were preserved. Second, many Christians on the extreme right see a fundamental opposition between the Bible and the Church, as if the former somehow had to be preserved from the latter. What they overlook is that the former had to be preserved *by* the latter. If the Church of the post-biblical period had not prepared copies of the biblical books, modern Christians would literally not have a Bible. Since the autographs do not survive, we are completely dependent on the labors of the post-apostolic generations. To put it more strongly, what we know the New Testament to say is what the manuscripts copied in the Early Church tell us it says. Naturally the earliest copyists of the biblical books did their best to be accurate, and textual critics tell us that we can be confident that we have a reliable Greek text of the New Testament, but again we see the basic point: the Bible and the Church should not be separated; both carry Christ's word to the world.

A. Textual Criticism

The task of the textual critic is to "establish" the text of a work for which a legible autograph does not survive. That is, he or she must learn which manuscripts contain the text, then evaluate the manuscripts to decide which ones should be considered basic for establishing the text, and then compare and collate the "readings" in the manuscripts to see the similarities and differences and to decide which reading is to be preferred. For example, if manuscript X has the verse, "Jesus said to his disciples," and manuscript Y has "he said to the disciples," the texual critic would ultimately have to decide whether the evangelist was more likely to have written "Jesus" instead of "he" or "the" instead of "his."

Superficially it seems the basic problem is that the autographs have not survived. Actually that is not really a great problem, because comparatively few autographs survive for any ancient work. For example, the works of Plato (d. 347 B.C.) survive mostly in Byzantine manuscripts of the Middle Ages, the earliest of which dates to 895 A.D., more than 1200 years after his death. The basic problem is actually that the manuscripts disagree with one another. For example, if the original of the Declaration of Independence were lost, and the only surviving copies dated to 1930 or later, but all the copies had the same reading, that is, "We hold these truths to be self-evident," etc., we would be confident that we were reading the text as it was originally written. The problem with the New Testament manuscripts is that they often do disagree, in much the way as the "Jesus" versus "he" example we just gave. The textual critic must decide which of the variant readings is the most reliable and thus the one most likely to correspond to the original.

To deal with these discrepancies, one must know how they occur, which is to say, how were manuscripts produced and what could go wrong in the production.

B. How Books Were Produced

The textual critic takes a different approach to a book from the rest of us. When we speak of a book, we mean its contents, for example, "That was a good book," or "That book was boring." But we often overlook that a book is first of all a physical object, something we must hold and open and look at and turn the pages of (and let fall to the floor when we fall asleep reading it). Although most of us see the physical nature of a book only in terms of the flashy or dull cover or of how many heavy books we must carry to class, the trained eye can see a lot more - the binding, the kind of printing, the quality of the ink and paper, and so forth. The textual critic must do this for ancient works, and in an age when all books had to be copied by hand, their physical nature was far more apparent.

Ancient writers used many materials, including clay tablets, stones, metals, potsherds, wood, wooden tablets with wax veneers, and even animal bones. Bibles were written on two surfaces, papyrus and parchment.

The papyrus plant, which gave English the word "paper," has grown on the banks of the Nile River for thousands of years. Ancient craftsmen would cut the long (12-15 feet) stems into six-foot sections and then split those sections into thin strips. They would next lay the strips on a flat surface with the fibers all going in the same direction, that is, either horizontally or vertically, and then glue to them another set of fibers at a right angle. When pressed together, the fibers made a reliable writing surface, especially on the horizontal side.

Parchment means treated animal skins, but the word itself is derived from Pergamum, a Greek city in Asia Minor

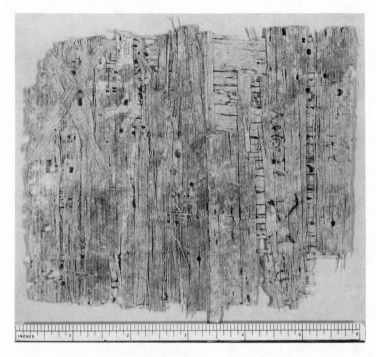

*Reverse of a parchment showing how strips of
papyrus were laid at right angles to form a writing edge.*

which developed this writing surface when papyrus from
Egypt was in short supply. Craftsmen would skin a dead
animal, scrape off all the hair from the skin, then wash and
pumice the skin on both sides, although the flesh side, that
is, the interior which never had hair on it, was usually the
better side. A fine, softer parchment called vellum was used
for deluxe editions.

Books were in two forms, the roll and the codex. The roll
consisted of sheets of papyrus or parchment stitched
together and then rolled around a wooden rod; one read the
book by unrolling it. The Latin word for something rolled
up is *volumen*, from which comes the English word

"volume." The rod was held by a knotted head. The term "head" came to mean the material on that particular roll, and if a book required several rolls, it was said to be on several heads. The Latin word for head is *caput*, from which comes the English word "chapter." Usually a roll was written on one side, but not always; the scroll in Revelation 5:1 has writing on both sides. Such a scroll is called an opistograph. If papyrus was the writing surface used for the roll, the writing would be on the horizontal fibers.

The roll was not easy to use, especially if one wanted to refer to an earlier passage, something the scripturally-minded Christians were fond of doing. Furthermore, the roll could not hold too much material without becoming excessively bulky. Scholars estimate that the two longest books in the New Testament, the Gospel of Luke and the Acts of the Apostles, would *each* require a roll thirty-two feet long. (Luke's decision to write a two-volume work may have been more than a theological one; a sixty-four foot role would have been extremely awkward if not actually impossible to use.) The Christians showed an early and enduring preference for the codex.

The codex is the ancestor of the modern book. At first the trunk of a tree (Latin: *caudex*) was split into tablets, and these were bound together at one end to make a book. Later this was done with sheets of papyrus and parchment, that is, the pages were grouped together and bound together at one end. The process has persisted until today, except that now paper is used.

Because Christians used books so heavily for their teaching and liturgies, they preferred the easy-to-use codex to the cumbersome roll. A survey of manuscripts from fourth-century Egypt shows that over 80% of the Christian works are codices.

These writing materials also provided us with a fundamental Christian word: Bible. The Greek writer Herodotus (*circa* 484-425 B.C.) refers to the papyrus plant as the *byblos*. A later writer, Theophrastus (370-285 B.C.), refers to the *biblos* and says that from this is made the *biblion* or papyrus book. The plural of this was *ta biblia*, the books.

Codex Vaticanus, a fourth-century uncial.

When Greek-speaking Christians referred to the Scriptures, they used the plural word *biblia*. The Latin-speaking Christians, however, treated *biblia* as a singular word (of the first declension), and *biblia* came to mean the collection of Scriptures or "Bible."

The person who actually did the writing was called a scribe, usually a man. Although educated people like Paul could write out their own works, many authors dictated to others, such as fellow disciples like Tertius (Romans 16:22), or professional scribes or slaves, and copies were almost always made by a scribe. He would choose the type of surface to write on, get a reed pen and ink, make a lined impression on the page to guide his pen, and then write. If the book were a codex, he would start on the right side or recto and then turn the page to the left side or verso. He could use one of two literary hands, or styles of writing, that is, rather large, rounded, capital letters called uncials or smaller letters called minuscule. (There was also the cursive or non-literary hand.) Following normal scribal practice, he would use no punctuation but would write a continuous text. He would, however, use abbreviations, an obvious necessity for copying books by hand. Often the scribe just copied the text as a whole, but occasionally he would divide the text into sections based on content, such as a particular parable or miracle story. This could be broken down even further, for example, he could end a line at a break in the sense of the text so that not all the lines were the same length; such a line was said to have been copied *per cola et commata*.

Another practical system for dividing lines is called stichometry. This was the usual practice of professional scribes. They were paid by the *stichos* or line of fifteen or sixteen syllables (approximately 34 to 38 letters). Since they were not paid for overruns, the scribes would usually stop at a *stichos* and go on to the next line. Scholars have computed the number of *stichoi* in various New Testament books; in round numbers, 2600 for Matthew, 1600 for Mark, 2800 for Luke, and 2300 for John.

C. Who Made the Surviving Copies?

Although we can accept our dependence upon copies, we can still wonder why we must rely on them at all. What happened to the autographs? Simply put, no one knows. We must assume that, for the most part, they were not deliberately destroyed. For example, communities founded by Paul or those receiving the Revelation from John would have treasured the originals, so they must have succumbed to accident or wear or harm by persecutors. Whatever the reasons, they are almost certainly irretrievably lost.

What about the surviving or extant copies? Where did they come from? The existence of copies depended upon the perceived value of the original. For example, if the first readers of Luke's gospel thought it of little worth - poorly written, boring, portraying Jesus badly and the like - no one would have bothered to copy it. But the first readers apparently valued it because the work was copied and made available to others. The same was obviously true for the other New Testament books, although it is unlikely that they were first copied because people considered them to be Scripture.

As we saw in an earlier chapter, throughout the second century these books grew in authority and came increasingly to be viewed as Scripture, which in turn meant that more individual churches wanted copies of them, and so more copies were made. Once the canon began to take shape, the books were routinely used in every community and their future survival was assured; there was no longer any chance that they would be lost for a lack of copies.

Complete New Testaments survive only from the fourth century, and only parts from earlier centuries, but there can be little doubt that some churches, especially the major ones like Alexandria, possessed complete New Testaments, although with the canon not yet settled, "complete" in the third century would necessarily include our twenty-seven books. In the fourth century, when the canon was largely settled and the Christians enjoyed the freedom to practice their faith and even imperial favor, many bibles were copied. Indeed, in 331, the Emperor Constantine personally ordered the copying of fifty parchment manuscripts of the Bible for the churches in his newly-founded capital city, Constantinople. This was truly an imperial command - imagine the entire Bible's being copied by hand fifty times - yet it now appears that not a single one of these survives, although scholars occasionally claim a particular manuscript to be one of them.

Extant copies of the New Testament occur in four forms: papyri, uncials, minuscules, and lectionaries. The papyri, which take their name from their writing surface, are usually

Codex Sinaiticus, a fourth-century uncial.

the earliest, but they are often in fragments, and they are used chiefly to correct or check up on a later text. Both the earliest fragment and the earliest complete book of the New Testament are papyri from Egypt.

The uncials are manuscripts, usually codices, written in those letters; since all the letters are capitals, these are occasionally called majuscules. The important ones date mostly from the fourth and fifth centuries, including the earliest complete New Testament, a fourth-century manuscript called the Codex Sinaiticus. The uncials form the basis of critical editions of the New Testament. Although lacking the very early dates of some papyri, in terms of the textual criticism of ancient texts, these are quite close to the originals. (Recall the manuscripts of Plato's work which date 1200 years and more after the author's death.)

Minuscules make up the third group; they too take their name from the type of hand used. These are usually later in date than the first two groups but often preserve ancient and unique readings. No serious scholar would overlook them.

Lectionaries are not New Testaments *per se*, but rather books of readings for liturgies. Naturally many of the readings are scriptural ones. In general these are quite late in date compared to the papyri and uncials, but they too occasionally preserve ancient and unique readings and can have value for the textual critic.

For particular scriptural passages, the scholar has recourse to the fifth source, scriptural quotations in the writings of Church Fathers; these, however, are used usually to verify readings from biblical manuscripts.

What has the search for manuscripts produced? The numbers are astonishing. In his *The Text of the New Testament* (pp. 32-33), Bruce Metzger says that there are a total of 81 Greek papyri, 266 uncial manuscripts, 2,754 minuscule manuscripts, and 2,135 lectionaries; a total of 5,236 manuscripts. Naturally most of these have limited value - usually to act as checks against the more important manuscripts - but they are there in phenomenal numbers. Compare the situation for the great Latin poet Catullus whose works survive in one Medieval manuscript; the great Old English epic poem *Beowulf* also survives in one manuscript and that has been badly damaged by fire. While we might still lament that we have lost the autographs of the New Testament, we can see that compared to other ancient books, it has a great many witnesses and is one of the most reliably established texts in history.

D. Evaluating the Evidence

Once the textual critic has catalogued and categorized the evidence, he or she must next decide which manuscripts should carry the most weight in preparing the edition. This can be very tricky business because of one undisputed fact: no manuscript, no matter how good it might be, is completely free from error. For a detailed description of how a manuscript is evaluated, Jack Finegan's *Encountering New Testament Manuscripts* is the best place to start; here I shall indicate what general processes the textual critics follow.

Scholars have to consider a manuscript's date, place of writing, the competence of the scribe, and the relation of the manuscript to others. This last point is the most complicated, so let us start there.

Suppose, for example, that we have five manuscripts, A, B, C, D, and E. Examination of them proves that B, C, and D were copied from A, and E was copied from B. Obviously B, C, and D are thus worth only as much as A and, in fact, less since their scribes have probably made mistakes in the copying of A. E is likewise worth only as much as B, and therefore less than A. This means that the editor does not have to work with all five manuscripts but only with A since the others are just copies of that or a copy of a copy of that. The editor should not ignore the other manuscripts' completely, but generally he or she can work without them.

Let us change the situation a bit. Suppose A were lost but the others survived. The editor could tell from reading B, C, and D that they have so many similarities that they were all based upon the same manuscript, but since the three also disagree with one another on a number of points, it is obvious that neither B nor C nor D was the exemplar for the other two, so therefore there must be some now lost manuscript (our A) from which all were copied. (E still occupies a low place as a copy of B.)

Let us make things even more complicated. Our manuscript A is still lost, but now B, C, and D have many copies. B has E, F, G, and H; C has K, L, and M; D has X, Y, and Z. The scribes of B, C, and D all made some mistakes when copying A, and naturally these mistakes were repeated by the scribes who copied B, C, and D. Furthermore, if copies were made of the copies and so forth, the mistakes would be repeated and repeated. The variant readings in B, C, and D would eventually give rise to three branches of the text. The word "branch" was not chosen at random, because when textual critics try to determine how a particular manuscript (such as A), whether surviving or lost, was the basis for a group of other manuscripts, they construct what is called a *stemma*, and they trace the spread of the manuscripts like the growth of a tree. From A came three branches, B, C, and D, and from them came E, F, G, etc. in a constantly growing profusion. The task of the critic is to follow the branches back to the root, to try to determine what A had to say. For an occasional verse, this is impossible, but for most verses it can be done. For example, if B, C, and D all say "Jesus said to his disciples," the editor can be sure that A said that since it is impossible that the scribes of B, C, and D would all make the same mistake in the same place.

Let us introduce just one more complication. We can tell from certain readings that the scribes of B, C, and D all copied from A, but suppose the scribe of C also checked with another ancient manuscript, Q, which is now lost and from which no copies were made. We can tell that C used A because of agreements with B and D, but we have no way to recognize the occasional odd reading coming from Q. If a pattern emerges, we might realize that C had access to another manuscript; if one does not, we might conclude that C simply has more mistakes than B or D.

Creation of a stemma demonstrates the relationships of manuscripts to one another and thus of their value relative to one another, but what about their value *per se*. Manuscript A might be the ultimate source of all those other manuscripts and thus crucial to determining how much value we should attach to the others, but how much is A itself worth?

In general, the earlier the manuscript, the better it is because the more a text is copied, the more likely it is that mistakes will creep in. Thus, a scholar working with two fourth-century uncials and a sixth-century minuscule, for example, would prefer the fourth-century witnesses to variant readings in the later witness. Should a second-century papyrus fragment survive, the scholar would check the fourth-century uncials against that for particular verses.

This approach is far from fool-proof. Suppose the second-century fragment were copied by a careless scribe and suppose the sixth-century minuscule were copied carefully from a reliable but now non-extant second-century manuscript. In this case, the latest of the four manuscripts would be the most valuable. But if a manuscript proves to be reliable and of an early date, scholars will always prefer it.

A second consideration is the place of copying. For example, if the author lived in Rome in the fourth century, and the textual critic had a sixth-century manuscript from Rome, he or she would be confident that the text was reliable because the author's works would be well-known in his own community and there is a good chance that the sixth-century copyist had access to the autograph or to a copy made directly from the autograph. Like the chronological criterion, this geographical one is reliable but not fool-proof.

This approach cannot be readily used with the New Testament since scholars cannot agree where most of the books were written, nor do manuscripts survive from the few places which have been agreed upon. But the geographical factor does play a role. In our discussion of the stemma, we saw that the repeated copying of a text can produce branches of the manuscripts which have particular readings. Scholars have determined that for the New Testament there are three major groups of manuscripts which preserve particular groups of readings, and these groups can be localized. Scholars call these groups "families;" the three chief families are the Alexandrian, the Western, and the Byzantine. Many scholars would claim that these designations are too broad, and that they should be broken down into smaller families; for now we will consider the general consensus. The names are to an extent artificial, because there was no historical situation in which a group of scribes set out to create an "Alexandrian" text, but rather scholars who first began to catalogue the manuscripts named the groups after the locations of the earliest members of that group to be discovered. Alexandrian means from the region of Alexandria, and Byzantine refers to the text used in Byzantium (also called the Koine or common text), but the name Western goes back to nineteenth-century editors who found the first examples of the family in Western manuscripts, such as ones containing Greek and Latin or in some Latin translations. Since then other "Western" manuscripts have been discovered in the Eastern Mediterranean, but scholars have kept the designation. Thus, although manuscripts can be localized by their readings, the localization is a very broad one.

The determinations of date, location and the relation of a manuscript to others still do not answer the basic question; how did the variations occur in the first place?. After all, the evangelist wrote "Jesus said to his disciples," not "He said to his disciples," to say nothing of variants like "The Lord Jesus said to his disciples" or "Jesus said to his apostles." What caused the ancient copyists to write something other than what the text said?

The earliest copyists would have tried to copy as accurately as possible, but a divine message does not guarantee the infallibility of the human copyist; purely human errors crept in. The textual critic must be aware of how these errors might have arisen, so that he or she can emend the text, that is, restore it to its most likely original reading. There have been cases in the history of the Church where theologians debated the meaning of a particular biblical passage and did so with a defective text. A better edition could have saved them a lot of trouble. Let us consider just a few general examples, remembering always that there is no guarantee which manuscripts will escape the ravages of history, and that any given manuscript could have been copied by an inept scribe.

Errors related to eyesight are most common. To copy a book, the scribe had to look at the exemplar, memorize a few words, turn to his still blank page or line, and write down those words. It sounds simple, but anyone who has ever copied more than a few lines from something like a classmate's notebook knows how troublesome it can be. Suppose the scribe had poor eyesight, especially in this age before the invention of spectacles. (In the eighth century there is a moving letter from Saint Boniface, apostle of Germany, to a friend in England asking for manuscripts with larger print because Boniface simply could not read the ones he possessed.) Suppose the light was poor or the original was illegible. Maybe two Greek letters looked alike, and the scribe mixed them up. If two lines ended with the same word (this is called homoteleueton), the scribe, who had to look away from the text to copy it onto a blank line, picked up the text again at the wrong line and so left out a line. Frequently a scribe would write the same word twice because he finished at the word, and when he began to copy again, he started with the same word; this is called dittography. The reverse is also common. The same word is used twice in the text in succession; the scribe, who has just written the word once, unconsciously goes on to the next, different word; this is called haplography.

Errors also arose from poor hearing. In the ancient world it was common to dictate a book to a group of scribes, and the problems related to this are just as serious as those related to copying by sight. Suppose the scribe was hard of hearing or simply had a cold which made it difficult for him to hear or was seated by a window so that street noises distracted him. Suppose the person dictating the text was a careless reader who left out words or who slurred. [Anyone who has ever taken notes in a classroom knows the difficulties and has the misfortune of seeing the results. Many students have told teachers that what they marked wrong on the students' tests in fact corresponded to what was in their notebooks, only to be told that their notes were incorrect.] Sometimes errors arise because words sound alike, such as "ladder" and "latter." In Revelation 4:3 the text reads "a rainbow that looks like an emerald," but some manuscripts have "priests" for "rainbow" because the two words sound alike in Greek. One can imagine how an exegete would handle a text like that.

Occasionally letters are transposed. As a teacher I have frequently seen "teh" for "the" on student papers, and the same thing happened to ancient copyists. Whole words and phrases also are transposed. (The following phrases are given to exemplify the process, but are not actual biblical phrases.) Often the transposition was harmless, such as "He will soon leave" becoming "He will leave soon," but think of "Only if he came" becoming "If only he came." Inevitably key words such as "not" were left out of certain verses.

Occasionally the scribe thought he was familiar with the text and so did not bother to read his exemplar carefully. Frequently in manuscripts of the Synoptic gospels scribes will put in one passage material from a parallel passage in another gospel, simply because the other passage was the better known. A prime example of this is the Lord's Prayer in Luke 11:2-4 which was harmonized with the longer and widely-used Matthean version (6:9-13). I have often proven the effect of memory on the text with Roman Catholic students by referring to the angel Gabriel's words at the Annunciation, "Hail, Mary, full of grace." In fact, the text (Luke 1:28) reads "Hail, full of grace;" many Catholics think the word "Mary" is there because of the well-known prayer.

It is clear that most alterations from the autograph were originally unintentional and easy to understand as human error, but for some manuscripts, it is obvious that the deviations were deliberate. Scribes would correct grammatical or syntactical errors, or they would add words that they thought should have been there, such as "the scribes" to Matthew 26:3 or the title "the Lord" before the name Jesus or "Christ" after it. Often they brought New Testament citations of the Old Testament into line with the Old Testament text.

Sometimes scribes changed the text to meet their own notions of Christian truth. For example, in Mark 13:32, Jesus says "But of that day or that hour, no one knows, not even the angels in heaven, nor the Son, but only the Father." This seemed to compromise Jesus' divine omniscience, so some scribes simply dropped the phrase "nor the Son." Other scribes, possibly wishing to honor Mary by eliminating a reading which would question her virginity, changed "his parents" in Luke 2:41 to "Joseph and Mary." But such intentional changes are easy to see and do not seriously hamper the textual critic's work.

The only way to finish this chapter is to ask the logical question: after all this work is done, do we know what the New Testament says? The answer is that we do and we don't. Textual criticism is never finished. First, new manuscripts are still being discovered. There have been widely-used printed editions of the Greek New Testament from the time of Erasmus' edition in 1516, but many important manuscripts were not discovered until the nineteenth or twentieth centuries. The papyrus fragment of John's gospel mentioned earlier was purchased from an Egyptian bookseller in 1920, but it was not recognized for what it is until 1934 when the British scholar C. H. Roberts discovered it among the papyrus collection of the John Rylands Library in Manchester. No one believes that all the papyri have been discovered (or for that matter, all the uncials, minuscules, and lectionaries), and when future finds come to light, they will have to be considered. Recall that the so-called Dead Sea Scrolls contain the Hebrew text of some biblical books in manuscripts almost 1, 000 years older than those previously known, and these scrolls were not discovered until 1947.

A second factor to consider is that all scholarly disciplines change. Not only is more knowledge gained, but the methods of gaining and interpreting knowledge change, too. These changes are often slow and unnoticeable, but they do take place. (Parents who look at their children's high school textbooks can immediately see how much has changed in the twenty years or so since they graduated.) Textual criticism is no different. New methods of investigation, new attitudes toward what is a reliable manuscript or an established text are always appearing. This is not a dead science which has established the New Testament text and then goes away. It is a living discipline which still has a role to play.

So we can say that while we have a reliable text of the New Testament text, we do not have a final one; texts and translations will continue to have the phrase "Other ancient authorities have" at the bottom of the page. But as much as we owe the textual critics, we also owe a great deal to our early Christian ancestors who preserved the text and guaranteed that we have anything at all to read.

7

"TEACH YE ALL NATIONS"

When the New Testament writers composed their books, they did what all writers do: they wrote in the language of their audience, in this case Greek. Greek was the language of the Early Christians because of the conquests of Alexander the Great (356-323 B.C.), who brought Greek rule and thus Greek language and culture to much of the Near East and even to parts of India. Greek became the dominant language of government and commerce in the Eastern Mediterranean, especially in the great cities founded by Alexander and his successors, the generals who divided his empire after his death. The best-known of these cities were Alexandria and Antioch, but there were many lesser ones as well. Recall how Paul and Barnabas were able to travel readily throughout Asia Minor because they spoke Greek. Although many people kept their native dialects (Acts 14:11), Greek became so pervasive in the cities that the Alexandrian Jewish community needed the Septuagint translation of the sacred books, and even the books of 1 and 2 Maccabees, which portray the heroic resistance of the Jews to the forced imposition of Hellenistic culture, were written in the language of the oppressors.

When the Romans took over the remains of Alexander's empire, they accepted the linguistic status quo and did not try to impose Latin on their Eastern subjects. Indeed, the

Greek language was no stranger even to the city of Rome itself. There were many resident foreigners who used it, and it is highly significant for the early history of the Church that almost all the literature associated with the Roman community in the first two centuries is in Greek: Paul's epistle to the Romans, Mark's gospel (if Rome were the place of writing), 1 Peter (5:13 implies Rome as the place of writing), possibly 2 Peter, Clement of Rome's epistle to the Corinthians, Ignatius of Antioch's letter to the Romans, the *Shepherd* of Hermas, the writings of Justin Martyr, and the letter of Bishop Dionysius of Corinth to Pope Soter, *circa* 170, preserved by Eusebius (*H.E.* 4, 23, 11). The Church expanded among a Greek-speaking populace, and the New Testament writers wrote in the language of the earliest Christians.

But Christianity was a religion for all persons, and it was preached and taught in a variety of languages. Jesus would have taught mostly in Aramaic, and the evangelization of the Palestinian Jews would have been mostly in that language as well, although no Aramaic Christian writings survive. Luke tells us that at Pentecost the disciples spoke in many languages (Acts 2:5-11), but this account actually intends to display God's power and to keep up the reversal-of-Genesis theme, that is, Jesus' resurrection undid the death Adam brought into the world and now the effects of the Tower of Babel were being reversed. It is uncertain when the Christian message was transmitted in a language other than Aramaic or Greek, but the many translations of the New Testament in the Early Church leave no doubt that it was.

I. The Value of the Translations

The translations have value for three groups of scholars, New Testament textual critics, philologists, that is, those who stude the origins and development of languages, and church historians.

How do translations, by definition at least one step away

from the Greek, help the textual critic who is trying to establish a Greek text? We saw in the last chapter that most of the manuscripts of the Greek New Testament date to the fourth century or later. Yet some of the translations, such as the Syriac and Latin ones, date to the second or third century (and, of course, later). This means that the first translators were working with manuscripts which had to be older than the now extant Greek ones, and they may preserve readings not found in Greek manuscripts or they may support readings found in them.

Inevitably the situation is more complicated. We do not possess the autographs of these first translations, and if we are looking at a fifth-century manuscript of a second-or third-century Latin or Syriac translation, we must recognize the likelihood of corruptions in the copying of the text. Textual critics allow for such possibilities and are thus able to bring translations into the general process of establishing a text.

Philologists have made great use of these translations for the understanding of ancient languages. In some cases, such as Latin, where a large body of literature exists, the New Tesatment versions allow us to see how the language was written and probably spoken at the time the translation was made. In other cases, where the surviving literature is scarce or late in date, such as Gothic or Armenian, the translations are of inestimable value as the earliest or most valuable or most extensive example of that language; frequently the translations combine two or even all of these characteristics. As the ancient societies gradually became Christian, the Bible in the vernacular was ever more widely used, and scholars can trace the Bible's influence on the development of a language.

[This is also true for modern languages. Scholars credit two factors for the development of modern German, the language of the imperial chancery in the late Middle Ages and Martin Luther's German translation of the Bible. The same applies, although perhaps not as extensively, to the Authorized Version of the Bible, better known as the King James Version, prepared in the early seventeenth century. A small way to gauge its pervasive influence even today is to note how newspaper crossword puzzles, when giving a clue for words like "thee" or "thou" or "thy," simply put "a biblical word."]

Church historians are the third group to use these transla-tions. To state the obvious, if there is a translation in a particular language, then Christianity had reached the peo-ple who spoke that language, and it had apparently enjoyed enough success among them to warrant a translation. This seems to say very little, but sometimes it can say a great deal. For example, we may have a translation but know little or nothing about how the Faith reached the people, and the translation is thus our only proof that it did. This type of evidence is similar to archaeological finds of Greek or Roman coins or pottery in places where no written histories tell us that Greeks and Romans went. Think also of the claims made from time to time about discoveries in North America of objects or markings supposedly related to Vik-ing explorers or Irish monks.

The translations provide the church historian with more than just proof that Christianity existed in a particular locale. They can tell us something about the people who produced them or about a shift in language speakers in a community (such as the third-century shift from Greek to Latin among the Roman community) or about a great historical event, such as Ulfilas' mission to the Goths.

Most important of all, the translations prove the determi-nation of God's people to make God's word available to all. Language can offer an obstacle to peoples; translations remove it. The ancient converts were probably both excited and comforted to hear or read Luke and Paul in their own language.

In general, the translations fall into two groups, those of languages spoken in the Eastern and more heavily Chris-tianized part of the Mediterranaen world and those of the Western part. We will begin with Eastern versions.

II. The Eastern Versions

A. Syriac Versions

As we know from Acts, Christianity spread rapidly in the Eastern Mediterranean, especially in those areas where Greek was spoken. This narrative is reinforced by Paul's letters to Eastern communities and by Revelation, written in Greek to seven communities in Asia Minor. Most scholars think the recipients of most of the gospels and the non-Pauline epistles also lived in the East. In Syria Antioch and its confines provided the center for Greek-speaking Christianity, but in the rest of the province most people spoke Syriac. When Christianity reached these people is uncertain. The legend of Abgar, the correspondent of Jesus, claims that the disciple Thaddeus evangelized the region, but there is no proof of Christianity's being in Syriac-speaking areas before the mid-second century. Jewish influence was strong in Syria, and during the reign of the emperor Claudius (41-54) the royal house of Adiabene converted to that faith. Jewish notions of monotheism and sacred scripture would have eased the way for Christianity. In the second century the Syriac church had an ecclesiastical organization and produced a theologian, Bardesanes.

The first Christian "scripture" in Syriac was not a scriptural book but rather the *Diatessaron*, Tatian's harmony of the four gospels mentioned in chapter four. Tatian, who loathed Greek culture, gave up his studies in Rome, where he had been the pupil of Justin Martyr, and about 172 he returned to the East where he is said to have founded the Encratites, an extreme ascetic group. He apparently composed the *Diatessaron* while still in Rome, but scholars dispute whether he wrote it originally in Syriac or in Greek and later translated it into Syriac. The work does not survive in Syriac, but scholars can detect it in gospel harmonies surviving in several other languages, including late revisions in Arabic, Persian, and even Flemish. The portions that survive prove how carefully Tatian had worked in the various strands of narrative.

Tatian's diligence and skill paid off. His work experienced great success and became the standard Syriac form of the gospels down to the fifth century. Tatian's countrymen rejoiced in a version of their own, even if it was not exactly a biblical book. We must remember that this occurred in the second century when the canon was still unsettled; furthermore, Tatian's version itself began to enjoy the status of a traditional text.

As long as Tatian was harmonizing the gospels, he decided to "improve" them in accordance with his ascetic views. He refrained where possible from referring to Joseph as Mary's husband; he changed the prophetess Anna's time of happy married life from seven years to seven days (Luke 2:36); and for Matthew 19:5, the verse "a man is joined to his wife" is put in the mouth of Adam and not of God. Drink went the way of sex. "I am the vine" of John 15:1 became "I am the tree of the fruit of truth;" the accusation that Jesus is "a glutton and drunkard" (Matt 11:19) is omitted from the text; and, on the cross, instead of being offered a mixture of wine and gall (Matt 27:34), Jesus is offered a mixture of vinegar and gall.

In the nineteenth century scholars discovered manuscripts of a Syriac version of the gospels (in the order Matthew, Mark, John, Luke) which was older than the standard Syriac New Testament, the Peshitta (to be discussed next), but independent of the *Diatessaron*. Later came discoveries of Acts and the Pauline epistles, but none of the Catholic Epistles and Revelation, which were disputed or rejected in the Syriac church canon. No one can be sure if this translation was an official response to Tatian's work or the result of independent efforts, but either way it reflects a reservations about the *Diatessaron* among the believers.

The relation of Christian life to a translation is very clear in the case of the Peshitta. In the fourth and fifth centuries the Syriac church came more and more into the mainstream of Eastern Christianity. Its liturgical use of a non-scriptural text prepared by a heretic became an increasing embarrassment. In the fifth century - and possibly as early as the late fourth - members of the Syrian hierarchy began the production of a new Syriac bible, later to be called the Peshitta or "simple version." Many scholars think this to be the work of Rabbula, Bishop of Edessa from 412 to 435. The Peshitta New Testament omits 2 Peter, 2-3 John, Jude, and Revelation, following the older Syriac canon and possibly reflecting the Antiochene canon of the early fifth century. The importance of this new version for the Syriac church is witnessed by the remark of Theodoret, Bishop of Cyrrhus in Syria from 423 to *circa* 466, that he found over 200 copies of Tatian in use in his province, and he replaced them with copies of the four gospels, presumably the Peshitta version. Tactics like this proved successful, and the new version became the standard one.

But for a while its success was in doubt. The Syriac church went into schism from most of the Greek-speaking (and all of the Western) churches in the fifth century. One group, the Monophysites or believers in only one nature in Christ, produced a version of its own in the sixth century. The translation was most likely done by one Polycarp at the urging of Bishop Philoxenus of Mabbug in northern Syria in 508. Philoxenus was one of the first great writers of the Monophysite church and a founder of the Jacobite sect of that church; the Jacobites became the national church of Syria and the so-called Philoxenian version of the Bible enjoyed great popularity there. Understandably this translation had little influence in non-Monophysite areas.

B. Coptic Versions

Coptic is the name for the language spoken by the rural natives of Early Christian Egypt. Greek was the language of Alexandria and the Hellenistic cities; outside those cities, Coptic, a descendant of the ancient Eygptian tongue, prevailed.

When Christianity reached Egypt is uncertain, but, as suggested in chapter two, if missionaries went to small towns in Asia Minor because those towns had Jewish communities, it is almost impossible to believe that no missionaries went to the great Jewish community of Alexandria. Apollos was from Alexandria (Acts 18:24), and many scholars think the epistle to the Hebrews may be from an Alexandrian milieu. The first solid evidence of Christianity in Egypt comes not from literary sources but from papyri fragments of the New Testament, the most important being the Manchester fragment of John's gospel. The *Epistle of Barnabas* dates to the first third of the second century and might be from Egypt. Pantaenus taught in Alexandria *circa* 180, and at end of the century Clement and Origen give proof of a flourishing church at Alexandria.

It is equally uncertain when Christianity moved into the rural areas and reached the Copts. When the emperor Decius persecuted the Christians in 250, the Egyptian martyrs included both Greeks and Egyptians, that is, Copts, according to Eusebius (*H.E.* 6, 41). This would imply that some preaching at least was in Coptic, and since the preaching would naturally center on the Bible, the preachers would probably have made some informal oral translations.

By the end of the third century an ascetic named Hieracas became the first Coptic native to write on biblical topics in his own language. In the late third and early fourth centuries, the monastic movement, led by Antony and Pachomius, two Coptic speakers, spread among the native Egyptians. *Circa* 320 Pachomius wanted members of his communities to be able to read the Psalms and Epistles, so obviously parts of the Bible had by then been translated into Coptic.

The word Coptic covers three major dialects and some lesser ones. It comes from the Arabic word for Egyptian. When the Arabs conquered Egypt in the seventh century, they probably did not distinguish among the language groups, which accounts for the breadth of the term. The three major dialects are Sahidic, Bohairic, and Fayyumic. The first was for a long time the language of much of Egypt and remained strong in the southern part of the country. Bohairic became the language of the Nile Delta, while Fayyumic centered on the Fayyum Oasis. Most Christian documents are in Sahidic. The Copts got their thirty-one letter alphabet by using twenty-four Greek uncials and seven letters from a native Egyptian script so they could express sounds which Greek could not convey.

Since the educated, urban, upper classes spoke Greek, Coptic became the vehicle for the less educated, rural classes. The earliest extant Coptic manuscripts date from the first half of the fourth century, and they are abundant from the fourth and fifth centuries generally. At this same time the Egyptian ascetics, mostly unlearned lay brothers, were composing the so-called *Sayings of the Fathers*, which embodied the practical and spiritual wisdom of the great desert *abbas*. Often accompanying these sayings was a Coptic account of Pachomius' life. Although these documents had to be translated into Greek and Latin to reach the wider Christian world - which they did with great effect - it is significant that in this period the Eygptian peasants had begun to speak with pride to the Greek-oriented outside world. It is no coincidence that the earliest manuscripts of the Coptic Bible appear at the same time. Both reflect Coptic pride and confidence vis-a-vis Alexandria.

[We will consider the New Testament and Christian art in chapter nine, but it is worth noting that decorative motifs in Coptic biblical manuscripts had great influence on Christian artists of other countries, even as far away as Ireland where the illuminators of the great manuscript the Book of Kells used Coptic techniques.]

C. The Armenian Version

During its long history Christianity became the official state religion of many countries. The first country to adopt Christianity as its national religion was Armenia, a small kingdom on the northeast frontier of the Roman Empire. Today the territory of this ancient kingdom is a part of the Soviet Union.

Tradition says the apostles Thaddeus and Bartholomew evangelized in Armenia. While this is not impossible, it has no historical foundation. Eusebius (*H.E.* 6, 46, 3) speaks of an epistle to the Armenians from Dionysius of Alexandria

(d. 264). Since there were enough Armenians to warrant a bishop (Eusebius says his name was Meruzanes) as well as a letter from an Alexandrian patriarch, Christianity must have reached the kingdom at least in the first half of the third century. The real founder of the Armenian church was Gregory the Illuminator (*circa* 257-331), an Armenian noble who was Christianized in Asia Minor and returned home as a missionary. He converted the king Tiridates, a one-time persecutor of the Church, and other important political figures. About 302 the king made Christianity the national religion, and soon many of the people had been baptized. Gregory destroyed one famous pagan shrine, turned another into a church, and in general kept up an active and fruitful career. He had helpers, usually fellow Armenians who had also been trained as Christians in other countries such as Syria or Greek-speaking Asia Minor. The first Armenian Christian books were in Greek or Syriac which the missionaries translated orally.

Like many small kingdoms caught between two large ones, Armenia lost its independence. Between 384 and 390 Persia annexed 80% of the country, with the rest going to Rome. The Persians tried actively to weaken Greek influences in Armenia, seeing them as links to the Roman enemy; this included the banning of Greek books. Having lost their political independence, the Armenians determined to preserve their cultural independence. This determination and the decrease of Greek influence stand behind the origins of a national Armenian literature. Leading the way were the *catholicos*, or primate, of the Armenian church Sahak (*circa* 350-439) and his associate, the monk Mesrop (*circa* 361-439). Building on the earlier work of a bishop named Daniel, in 406 Mesrop created an Armenian alphabet of thirty-six letters, borrowing mostly from the Greek but also from the Syriac alphabet. About 410 he produced an Armenian New Testament; by 414 he and Sahak had translated the Old Testament as well. Scholars still debate about the amount of Greek versus Syriac influence in the Armenian version.

Although other works were translated into Armenian and

indigenous works began to appear, the Armenian Bible made the newly-written language popular. The people took great pride in their creation and called it the "Queen of the Versions" because the translators elaborated upon the text and made some of the readings more colorful. For example, in Mark 7:25, the little girl was not "possessed" by an unclean spirit; rather she was "squeezed" by one. "The crowd" of John 7:49 became "this riotous crowd." Bruce Metzger observes, "the version, by introducing in some degree the work of commentator as well as that of translator, provides the reader with the generally faithful and idiomatic rendering praised for its clarity and dignity of expression." (*The Early Versions of the New Testament*, p. 163)

It also provided the reader with something else. Its canon includes the apocryphal letter of the Corinthians to Paul as well as his third epistle to them.

D. Other Eastern Versions

Adjacent to Armenia was the kingdom of Iberia, later known as Georgia and now lying wholly within the Soviet Union. Tradition credited a captured Christian slave woman named Nino with the bringing of the faith to Georgia in the fourth century. The country did become heavily Christianized in that century, and in the next the Georgians invented an alphabet and produced books in their own language. Armenian tradition credits its own Mesrop with giving the Georgians an alphabet. By the middle of the fifth century at least parts of the New Testament had been translated. Scholars argue as to which New Testament was the basis for the translation; Greek, Syriac, Armenian, or some mixture of these are the candidates. The Georgian canon did not include Revelation. In the tenth century, when whe Georgian church was in contact with the Byzantines, a great spiritual figure named Euthymius revised the Georgian translation and included Revelation in the canon.

Christianity may have reached the Romanized areas of

Arabia by the second century. It was definitely there by the third when Origen made two trips to Arabia to discuss Christian doctrine. In the fourth century missionaries from both the Roman areas and from Ethiopia across the Red Sea reached the nomadic tribes and made some conversions. This missionary work did not, however, result in an Arabic translation of the New Testament. That had to wait until the Islamic Arabs took over the region. Traditions credit several people with the first translation, but no one dates it earlier than the seventh century even if the traditions are historically reliable. Arabic versions exist in translation from Greek, the Peshitta, and Coptic versions.

Acts 2:9 says that there were "Parthians and Medes" among the apostles' audience at Pentecost, but Christianity apparently did not reach Persia until the third century. It was definitely there in the fourth. When Christianity became the religion of the Roman emperors, the Persian kings began to suspect their Christian subjects of disloyalty. The king Shapur II (309-379) vigorously persecuted them. But the Persian church, well founded by Bishops Papa and Shem'on (who died a martyr in 344 or 345) survived. In 484 it broke with the Greek church to become Nestorian, that is, to follow the teachings of Nestorius (died *circa* 451) on the person of Christ. Nestorian Persian missionaries reached China in the seventh century. The first translation of the New Testament into Persian dates to the early fifth century, but this is known only from second-hand sources. As Metzger succinctly puts it, "Of the Scriptures (in the vernacular), not a page of the New Testament is known today..." (*Early Versions*, p. 276).

In later centuries Christian missionaries reached other Asian peoples. A version of the New Testament from the ninth century survives in Sogdian, a Central Asian language, and there is evidence of versions for the Albans of the Caucasus, the Huns, and the Chinese, the last being the work of Nestorian missionaries.

E. The African Versions

Under the general heading of Eastern versions fall two African versions, Ethiopian and Nubian.

All readers are familiar with the story of Philip's conversion of the Ethiopian eunuch in Acts 8:26-39, but Ethiopian tradition asserts a much older biblical link, namely, that the Queen of Sheba who visited Solomon (1 Kings 10:1-13) was an Ethiopian. Furthermore, she bore him a son, Menelik, who was educated at Jerusalem. We must judge this account, which includes much more, a legend, but it does reflect the historical fact that Semitic invaders from Arabia entered Ethiopia sometime between 1000 and 400 B.C. Ethiopian, or Ge'ez, is a Semitic language, although it is written from left to right, unlike other Semitic scripts.

The eunuch of Acts was not the only New Testament personage credited with introducing Christianity to Ethiopia. Various sources claim that the apostles Matthew and Bartholomew and Andrew all evangelized there. The best historical evidence places the introduction of Christianity into Ethiopia in the fourth century when Frumentius, a captured, enslaved Christian from Tyre, won favor with his masters and managed to convert the king and his family. Frumentius went to Alexandria where he met Athanasius, who had him consecrated bishop and spiritual leader of the Ethiopian church. This traditional account is supported by archaeological and numismatic evidence for the Christian faith of the fourth-century king Ezana. The Ethiopian church remained in contact with the Alexandrian church well into the fifth century when Egyptian and Syrian Monophysite refugees from Byzantine persecution fled to Ethiopia, where they helped to evangelize the remaining pagan areas. Nine Monophysite monks, apparently Syrians, evangelized so successfully that they are known in Ethiopian tradition as the Nine Saints. These nine, who prepared liturgies and wrote theology in Ge'ez, also made the first vernacular translations of the Bible in the late fifth or early sixth century.

Over 300 Ethiopian manuscripts of the New Testament are extant, but most are of the sixteenth century or later and many contain beautiful illustrations to accompany the text. There is one manuscript from the tenth century, and two from the eleventh. The translation shows the influence of several other versions, including Greek, Syriac, and Arabic, although the first translations, now non-extant, would have been from Greek or Syriac.

Nubia, divided into three small kingdoms, lay between Egypt and Ethiopia; today it is the Sudan. The Romans used the Nubians to guard southern Egypt against nomadic desert tribes. By the early fourth century Christianity had reached the nearest of the three kingdoms at the city of Philae near the modern Aswan High Dam, but the effective Christianization of Nubia occurred in the sixth century. According to the Monophysite historian John of Ephesus, the orthodox Byzantine emperor Justinian (527-565) and his Monophysite wife Theodora (d. 548) each arranged for a mission to Nubia to win support for their respective causes. Whether or not this was the case, Christianity made large gains in the kingdoms, and apparently both survived in Nubia until the end of the fourteenth century when, under Arab pressure, the population converted to Islam.

Scholars believe that the Nubians or foreign missionaries would have made a translation of the Bible into the vernacular in the sixth century, but the earliest manuscript dates to the eleventh century. Even that is not of a biblical book but of a lectionary, a bare fragment from an African church with centuries of history.

III. The Western Versions

A. The Latin Versions

In Christian history Latin easily claims the title of the most important Western language. It became the language of the Western European churches down to the Reformation and for the Roman Catholic countries until the Second

Vatican Council (1962-1965). The roster of great Christians who wrote in Latin includes not only ancient and Medieval writers but also Reformation figures such as Martin Luther and John Calvin. The creators of the earliest Latin versions wished to solve an immediate problem, the conversion and evangelization of Latin-speakers; they could never have imagined what kind of future Christianity would have in their language.

But as we saw earlier in this chapter, the Roman Christian community of the first and second centuries relied upon Greek. This suggests many of its members were resident foreigners. The same situation prevailed for the Roman Jews; most Jewish grave inscriptions from this period are in Greek. Obviously the Church converted some Latin-speaking pagans, and the Christian proclaimers would have used Latin to achieve this, but Latin did not replace Greek. Even the pontificate of Pope Victor I (*circa* 189-198), a Latin-speaking African, did not alter the situation.

A further proof of the strength of Greek is that some Latin-speaking Jews in the vicinity of Rome had made vernacular translations of many of their biblical books. This means that the Christians could have read at least parts of the Old Testament in Latin, and they must surely have considered the possibility of translating the New Testament. But Greek persisted.

This has led many scholars to think Christian Latin began in North Africa. Because that region now belongs so firmly to the Arab world, we do not often think of it as ever having been Western, but Roman Africa was one of the Empire's most important Western provinces. Although many inhabitants spoke native Berber dialects and others spoke Greek, Latin was the dominant language there. Christianity certainly reached Rome before it reached Africa, but the southern shore of the Mediterranean offers the first proof of the New Testament in Latin.

About 180 a Roman proconsul in Carthage put several citizens from a village called Scilli on trial for being Christians. In the course of the trial, he asked one of them what was in the box he was holding. The Scillitan Christian replied, "Books and letters of Paul, a just man." Since these African villagers would have lacked the education to read Greek, the Pauline letters must have existed in a Latin version by this time. Furthermore, it is difficult to believe that Paul's letters were available but no account of Jesus himself was; most likely at least one or two gospels had also been translated. Two African writers, Tertullian (*circa* 160-*circa* 220) and Cyprian (d. 258) leave no doubt of a Latin New Testament in their province by the early third century.

As for Rome, the Latin Muratorian Canon implies the existence of a Latin New Testament about 200, and by the middle of the century the theologian and anti-pope Novatian (d. 258) cites the New Testament passages in Latin.

As usual, the first translations are not extant, nor can we say who made them. Augustine remarked in his book *De Doctrina Christiana* (2, 16) that anyone who had a Greek manuscript of the New Testament and thought he could translate made a translation. While he has certainly exaggerated, no one is sure by how much. Probably the translations were at first semi-official, but when they were used for liturgical purposes official translations would be required.

These ancient translations fall under the heading *Vetus Latina* or Old Latin, to distinguish them from the *Vulgata Latina* or Vulgate, which we will consider next. There is no actual Old Latin text *per se*. Scholars identify two major versions, the African and European, and many would break the second one down into South Gallic and Italian versions. The current evidence indicates that no one person ever translated all twenty-seven books. Several dozen Old Latin manuscripts survive, including some from the fourth century. All New Testament textual critics use this very important source in establishing the Greek text.

The immediacy of the Old Latin, its "colloquial and sometimes vivid, down-to-earth character" (Metzger, *Early Versions*, p. 324), helped to popularize it and guarantee its success. This vernacular Bible brought a host of new words into the Latin language. Some Greek words were simply Latinized; *apostolos* became *apostolus*, *diakonos* became *diaconus*. Other Latin words were neologisms, that is, newly-made words, such as *sanctificare* and *revelare*, in cases where the Greek could not be adapted. Since Latin formed the basis of the modern Romance tongues and since it had great influence on non-Romance tongues, terms like these passed almost unnoticed into the modern vernaculars, such as the English words deacon and revelation.

Because of the diversity and occasionally the disparity of the translations, all sorts of traits appear in Old Latin manuscripts. For example, some follow the so-called Western order of the gospels, that is, Matthew, John, Luke, and Mark, and are thus related to the Western text. The influence of Tatian's *Diatessaron* appears in several gospel manuscripts, including ones as late at the sixth century, while Marcion's influence shows up in other codices.

If the situation of the Old Latin manuscripts seems confused to us today, we can imagine the effect it had on those who had to use them for worship or exegesis. In 383, someone decided to do something about it. Pope Damasus I (366-384), an energetic and forceful proponent of Latin culture, especially vis-à-vis the Greek churches, asked the great scholar and Latinist Jerome (*circa* 348-*circa* 420) to revise the existing translations by consulting the Greek originals, including the Septuagint for the Old Testament. The condition of the text appalled Jerome. In the preface to his version of the gospels, he passed the famous remark that there were almost as many versions as manuscripts. Undaunted, he stuck to his task and in 384 produced a revision of the gospels, not a new translation from the Greek. Some people found these unfamiliar Latin gospels offensive, but Jerome defended his work vigorously and even harshly.

In that same year Damasus died. Jerome, an ascetic, had earlier levelled some vulgar criticisms at the supposedly luxury-loving Roman clergy. With his papal protector gone, Jerome's enemies forced him to leave Rome. Accompanied by some wealthy women friends, he settled in Bethlehem, never to return to the imperial capital. In the Holy Land he continued what was to be his greatest achievement, the revision of the rest of the New Testament and the

translation from the Hebrew original of much of the Old
Testament. (He once translated the Psalms from the Septuagint as well.) His version had difficulty winning acceptance during his lifetime, but some great writers of the Early
Middle Ages, such as Cassiodorus (*circa* 480-*circa* 575) and
Pope Gregory I the Great (590- 604) used it. By the eighth
century it was the dominant Latin version. By the end of the
Middle Ages it was known as the Vulgate or common
version because everyone used it.

The Vulgate's triumph did not drive the Old Latin from
the field. Some biblical books in one of those versions
survive from the twelfth and even the thirteenth century.
Mixed versions, that is, Vulgate manuscripts with Old Latin
readings, abound. But the Vulgate was the basic text.

In the previous chapter we saw how a text from one
century and place can survive in a manuscript from a different century and a very different place. The Vulgate illustrates this well. In the seventh century Irish missionaries from
the island monastery of Iona and Roman missionaries sent
by Gregory the Great began the evangelization of the pagan
Anglo-Saxons in Great Britian. By the early eighth century
most of the English had converted. A northern English
abbot named Ceolfrith had his monks prepare three complete Vulgates, one of which he planned to present as a gift
to Pope Gregory II when he visited Rome. Ceolfrith never
finished the trip, dying along the way in France, but his
companions brought the manuscript on to Italy for him. It
eventually found a home in the Cistercian monastery of St.
Salvator at Monte Amiata. Known now as the Codex Amiatinus, it came to its current home in the Laurentian Library
in Florence in 1786. In the course of time, all earlier complete Vulgates were lost. This, combined with the quality of
the scribal work in Amiatinus, has made this Anglo-Saxon
codex the foremost authority in establishing the Vulgate
text. Jerome, like a true fourth-century Roman, thought
northern Britain a wasteland inhabited by ignorant barbarians. How ironic that his translation is best preserved in a
"barbarian" manuscript.

The Old Latin deserves credit for getting Christians to

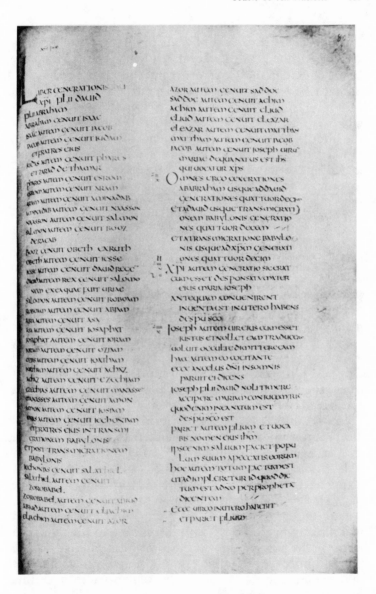

Codex Amiatinus, the most important manuscript of the Latin Bible — eighth-century English.

write in Latin, but the Vulgate is the Bible all the later Latin-speakers read. It survives in more than 10,000 manuscripts. All the great Medieval theologians understood the Word of God in the words of Jerome. Because ecclesiastical authorities frowned upon vernacular translations, such translations were few in number, and the Vulgate was usually the Bible read even by the great vernacular authors of the Middle Ages. Its influence extended beyond the writers; visual artists and musicians also used it in their creations, including the stained glass and statuary of the great Gothic cathedrals and liturgical chants and masses. The effects of the Vulgate on the intellectual and cultural history of Western Christianity are, in a word, incalculable.

B. The Gothic Version

From the point of view of the historian, the existence of a Latin version was inevitable. Any successful religious movement originating in the Roman Empire would sooner or later arrive in the capital where the local situation would, again sooner or later, demand a translation of its sacred writings. But the Gothic version was far from inevitable. It owes its existence to one man, whose story even today has touches of romance and excitement.

In the third century tribes of Germanic barbarians called Goths made raids into the Roman territory of Cappadocia in Asia Minor and brought back booty and slaves. About 311, a boy named Ulfilas ("Little Wolf") was born to a Cappadocian Christian mother and probably a Gothic pagan father. Christians were allowed to practice their faith among the largely pagan Goths and some evangelization had already occurred, so Ulfilas was able to function as a lector in the community. At this time he began to translate the Scriptures into Gothic, almost certainly starting with oral presentations. *Circa* 338 he took part in a Gothic mission to Constantinople. While there he became acquainted with Arianism, the doctrinal position that the Son of God is neither equal nor consubstantial with the

Father in the Trinity. The Arian bishop Eusebius of Nicomedia, then bishop of Constantinople, recognized the young man's abilities and had him consecrated bishop of the Goths, probably in 341.

Ulfilas returned home where he completed his translation of the Bible, except for the Books of Kings because he felt the Goths had enough warlike proclivities and did not need encouragement from the Bible. He also evangelized further until a pagan reaction set in and a persecution of the Christian broke out in 347. With members of his community he fled to Roman territory; whether he later returned to the Goths is uncertain. He died about 381 in Constantinople. Although not the first missionary to his people, Ulfilas alone has earned the title "Apostle of the Goths" because he made the Word of God permanently available to his people.

The Goths had no alphabet, so Ulfilas invented one using Greek and Roman letters and some Gothic runic elements. He made a very literal, almost word-for-word translation from the Greek, following Greek word order even at the expense of Gothic idioms. The version was accordingly stilted, but, most importantly, it was there. Germanic barbarians on the Roman frontier had a Bible and a written language.

Most Goths eventually became Arian Christians, and when they spread their empire to Italy and Spain, Ulfilas' translation became widely known. Unfortunately almost all manuscripts of the Gothic version are now lost; no Gothic version survives for Acts, Hebrews, the Catholic Epistles, or Revelation. The best manuscript is the sixth-century Codex Argenteus, the Silver Codex, which contains the gospels; a fragment of Luke also dates from the sixth century. Other Early Medieval Gothic manuscripts are palimpsests, that is, written-over manuscripts. Someone who wished to write or copy a book pumiced over the Gothic text and then wrote on the newly-cleaned page. But modern ultraviolet photography has enabled scholars to restore the original Gothic text.

Ulfilas' Gothic Bible is not only the first Gothic writing but also the most important for the understanding of that ancient language. Rarely can the effect of the Bible on a people's culture be seen so clearly.

C. *Later Western Versions*

The Latin and Gothic versions are the only Western ones from the Early Christian period. In the Early Middle Ages the conversion of Western Europe resulted in several more versions. About 860, two Greek brothers from Thessalonica, Methodius and Constantine, did missionary work among pagan tribes near the Sea of Azov, just north of the Black Sea. In 863 they began a new mission, this time to the Slavic tribes of Eastern Europe. Apparently Constantine, an accomplished linguist, began immediately to make a translation of some liturgical books into Slavonic. The brothers' work among the Slavs took them from Byzantine into Roman ecclesiastical jurisdiction. East German bishops looked unfavorably upon these new missionaries who wished to establish a Slavic church free of German control, but Popes Hadrian II and later John VIII supported the brothers, although insisting that the Scripture readings in the liturgy be read first in Latin and then in Slavonic. In 868, when the brothers visited Rome, Constantine became terminally ill. He took monastic vows and a new name, Cyril, the name by which he is best known. He died early in 869. Methodius returned to work again among the Slavs until his death in 885.

Cyril and Methodius both evangelized, but to Cyril alone goes the credit for creating the Slavonic alphabet. He did not, however, invent the Cyrillic alphabet but rather the Glagolitic, which consists of 38 letters. The alphabet known as Cyrillic came into being early in the tenth century. Old Church Slavonic, as this language is called, is yet another example of the Bible's originating an alphabet and thus a literature.

Also in the ninth century - or possibly even in the late eighth - an anonymous translator turned Matthew's gospel into Old High German from a Latin original. About 830 a

German version of the *Diatessaron* appeared, based upon a sixth-century Latin manuscript of Tatian's work. In that same century a German poet composed his own gospel harmony, while another wrote an epic poem based upon the *Diatessaron*.

Finally, we will see what were the earliest versions in our native tongue. The Anglo-Saxon church historian Bede (673-735) tells of the herdsman Caedmon who paraphrased the Genesis creation story in Old English. Bede himself rendered at least parts of John's gospel in the vernacular, the first known English translation of a New Testament book. Alfred the Great (849-901) translated some of Acts. Ironically the first substantial translation was not intended as a translation at all but rather as an aid to readers of Latin. About 700 Bishop Eadfrid of Lindisfarne copied out an *evangelium*, that is, a book containing the four gospels in Latin. Its beautiful decorations and illustrations, which follow Irish artistic precepts, made the manuscript famous as the Lindisfarne Gospels. In the mid-tenth century a priest named Aldred oversaw an interlinear translation into English, that is, the translation was written above the lines of Latin text. About the same time other English scribes were making an interlinear translation of an Irish *evangelium*, the MacRegol gospels, which was written about 800. By the second half of the tenth century some English Bendictine monks had made a free, Old English translation of all the gospels.

Although English translations began in the Anglo-Saxon period, modern English versions derive ultimately from Late Medieval ones, such as that of John Wycliffe (d. 1384) and his circle.

8

SPIRITUALITY AND ART

In the previous chapters we saw how the New Testament books came to be written, how the Church distinguished which belonged in the canon and which did not, how we know what the text actually says, and how the message reached the first generations of non-Palestinian Christians. In this chapter we will look at the final stage in the formation of the New Testament, its acceptance by the people.

Throughout this book we have tried to relate the New Testament to the life of the Church. Here we will examine its effects on Early Christian spirituality and art, both of which were the property of the whole community. We will not consider the early exegesis of the New Testament which, after Origen, depended heavily upon allegory, that is, the assumption that the literal meaning of a text is but a pointer to the "real" meaning. Although the allegorists produced an impressive and valuable body of literature, it rarely drew from the life of the people. The same is true for the so-called Antiochene school which emphasized the historical and literal meanings of the text. Exegetes of both groups, however, produced many homilies based upon from their exegesis, although in these we see them trying to interpret for the community rather than drawing from it. For the community's experience of the New Testament, we do better to restrict ourselves to the spirituality and the art.

I. Spirituality

Spirituality is often a difficult topic to study because it can be so intensely personal, as, for example, daily prayer. But there are some aspects of spirituality which transcend the personal and which can characterize an age. Although there were many forms of spirituality in the Early Church, we will concentrate on two forms which arose in the first centuries and which found their fullest expression then: martyrdom and monasticism. Few Christians were either martyrs or monks or both, but these people captured the imagination of all Christians. The martyrs and the monks were the ideal Christians, those who showed what the rest could do. In locales like North Africa, martyrdom was widely thought to be a Christian duty should the opportunity arise, and in the fourth and fifth century the Church at large was permeated with the monastic spirit and by bishops who had either been monks or who had practiced a monastic life-style with their clergy. Significantly, the New Testament influenced heavily both martyrdom and monasticism.

A. Martyrdom

Of all the elements of Early Christian history, none catches the popular imagination quite like martyrdom. Although there were cases where Jews martyred Christians and, in the later Empire, where Christians put other Christians to death for heresy, the real story lies in the conflict between Christianity and the pagan Roman Empire. It is a genuinely amazing story, of Christians dying for the faith at the hands of mobs, governors, and emperors; of ordinary women and men staunchly enduring all sorts of indignities and tortures to defy the most powerful state of the ancient world; of victims being the true victors. There were inevitably less than heroic instances of Christians who apostasized or who bribed their way out of persecution, but in general the lines are clear. The Christian martyrs stood up to the might of Rome and won. To cite the familiar translation of some words of Tertullian in his *Apologeticum* (ch. 50), "The blood of the martyrs is the seed (of the Church)."

1. Martyrdom in the New Testament

In Greek the word *martyros* means a "witness," but in Christian circles the word came to mean one who gave the ultimate witness with his or her life. Christian martyrdom antedated the New Testament. Ancient Christians considered Jesus to be a type of martyr since he died for his teaching. The post-resurrection community counts Stephen (Acts 6:8-7:60) as its protomartyr. Acts also tells us that Paul, who watched Stephen die and approved of it, himself came close to death several times because of his fearless preaching of the Word, for example, Acts 14:19, 19:23-41, and 23:12-35. In 2 Cor 11:23-26 Paul, too, refers to the dangers he faced. Acts also makes it clear that Christians faced lesser punishments, such as flogging, for example, Acts 5:40-41, 16:16-24.

Revelation 2:13 mentions an Antipas who died for the faith, and, of course, the entire book deals with the conflict between the forces of good and evil and contains several references to martyrdom, such as 11:7-10, 12:17, and 13:7. Other New Testament passages refer to unspecified troubles caused by outsiders, for example, 1 Thes 2:14-15, 2 Thes 1:4, James 1:2, Hebrews 10:32-39. For the post-apostolic Christians, their sufferings followed those of both their Lord and their earliest ancestors in the Faith.

But there was more at stake than just historical precedent. Although no Christian - not even Jesus (Luke 22:42) - wished to suffer, it was widely and quickly accepted that suffering would be an almost inevitable part of Christian life. The necessity of Jesus' suffering occupies a central place in all four gospels. The Synoptics all record three predictions of his passion (Mark 8:30-33, 9:30-32, 10:32-34; Matthew 16:21-23, 17:22-23, 20:17-19; Luke 9:22, 9:44-45, 18:31-34). Even John, who, as noted earlier, did not care to emphasize the passion, acknowledged that Jesus had to die to accomplish his task, for example, John 10:14-18.

This principle of the necessary suffering of Jesus soon produced an important corollary, the necessary suffering of his disciples. In Mark 10:38 Jesus asks the sons of Zebedee, "Can you drink the cup that I must drink, or be baptized with the baptism with which I must be baptized?" As we just saw, Acts and the epistles witness that many Christians did indeed drink from that cup. Moreover, they began to see their endurance of suffering as a good thing. When Paul recounted his trials in 2 Cor 4:7-12 and 11:21-29, he sorrows that he must boast of what he has endured but this proves that he has been a good and faithful apostle. More succinct are the words of Luke about the reaction of Peter and John to their flogging at the orders of the Sanhedrin. "Then they left the presence of the council, rejoicing that they were counted worthy to suffer dishonor for the name" (Acts 5:41).

The spirit of the apostolic age in no way diminished in the next generations; indeed, as the persecutions became more severe, the Christian response became stronger. Many accounts of the martyrs survive in invaluable documents such as Roman court records and in accounts written by Christians for the edification of other Christians. These have been conveniently collected and translated by the late Herbert Musurillo, S.J., and the reader can find them in his book, *The Acts of the Christian Martyrs*. We will consider just a few of the more prominent accounts to see how the New Testament affected the Christian understanding of martyrdom.

2. Polycarp

The earliest extant account of a Christian martyrdom is that of Saint Polycarp, bishop of Smyrna, author of an epistle, recipient of a letter from Ignatius of Antioch, and, according to tradition, an acquaintance of the apostles.

Circa 156 he was burned to death for being a Christian in the city of Smyrna. Members of the church there wrote an account of his execution at the request of the church of Philomelium. The *Martyrdom of Saint Polycarp*, as it is known, refers to the New Testament throughout.

The prologue cites Jude 2, and the first paragraph, which justifies the deaths of Jesus and Polycarp, cites Philippians 2:4. Polycarp has a vision of his death (para. 6). He awaits his persecutors and makes no attempt to escape arrest once he had been betrayed (cf. Matt 26:47-56). The police chief who arrests Polycarp was named Herod, and those who betrayed him are compared to Judas. Like Jesus the bishop first confronts his accusers with silence and then speaks only a few words (para. 8). Before he is burned, he prays to God, and his prayer includes citations from Revelation and the Gospel of John, both well-known in Asia (para. 14). After his death, an executioner pierces his side, and so much blood flows out that it extinguishes the smoldering flames (para. 16).

Scholars debate how much of this account is history and how much pious embroidery, but for our purposes, there is no doubt that New Testament motifs played a great role in the community's understanding of Polycarp's heroic death.

3. *The Martyrs of Lyons*

In the year 177, while the philosopher-emperor Marcus Aurelius ruled Rome, a vicious persecution broke out against the Christians in the Gallic city of Lyons. The Christians were largely foreigners from Asia Minor, and the fear of an oriental cult's polluting the local worship may have added to the blood-crazed brutality of the mob, which thronged to see the executions. When the storm had passed, the Christians at Lyons wrote an account of the persecution for the churches of Asia to tell them how their brethren had suffered but persevered. The account makes chilling but exciting reading; New Testament citations and motifs appear throughout. [The letter is preserved in chapters one and two of book five of Eusebius' *History*.]

The authors attribute the persecution to the work of the devil, and when they initially describe the martyrs' resistance, they make references to Romans, Hebrews, and 1 Timothy. The accounts of the individual martyrs include apt citations to Matthew, Luke, John, Acts, 2 Corinthians, Galatians, 1 Timothy, James, and 1-2 Peter. In all, thirteen books of the eventual canon are cited.

One martyr, Blandina, is hanged on a stake in the form of a cross and exposed to wild animals, but no beast attacks her, so her fellow Christians picture her, like Jesus, as having defeated the devil. When another martyr, Sanctus, is burned alive, the account says he was "cooled and strengthened by the heavenly fountain of water that flows from the side of Christ" (Musurillo, *Acts*, p. 69). The reference is to John 19:34, and it works upon the theory of opposites, that is, the pains of the flames are extinguished by the water of Christ. (It may also refer to the flames of hell being obviated by the waters of baptism.) Yet this same image appears in the *Martyrdom of Saint Polycarp*, and it is likely that second-century Christians used particular New Testament verses to understand martyrdom.

The point is made throughout the letter that these martyrs stand in a glorious tradition going back to Jesus and his first disciples.

4. Perpetua and Felicity

The anonymous *Passion of Saints Perpetua and Felicity* is probably the best-known of all the accounts of the martyrs. It comes from a Montanist circle in North Africa and from the early third century; it portrays the spirit-filled martyrs standing up defiantly to their pagan persecutors. The Christians will fight by dying, but there is no doubt that they will triumph. Three martyrs tell the mob, "You have condemned us, but God will condemn you" (para. 18).

Replete with visions of heaven, conflict between father and daughter, separation of mother and child, and open defiance of a persecution, the *Passion* was widely popular in the Latin West.

Like the accounts of Polycarp and the martyrs of Lyons, it often refers to the New Testament. It includes direct citations from Acts and 1 John and clear references to Luke, Romans, 1 Corinthians, and, understandably, Revelation. Perpetua, the central character, is a Christ-figure: she must leave her bodily family to do God's will; in a vision she cures her dead brother of face cancer; she battles and conquers the devil in a one-to-one encounter; she dies for her beliefs.

Yet the subtlest use of the New Testament occurs in the account of a Christian named Saturus. A wild leopard bites him. His own blood so drenches him that the mob shouts ironically, "Well-washed!," a form of greeting to be used in the public baths which many Christians considered breeding grounds for immorality. But the anonymous author calls this drenching with blood a second baptism, recalling Jesus' words in Mark 10:38 about being "baptized with the baptism with which I must be baptized." Since Christians being baptized usually wore white robes for the ceremony, the word "wash" probably recalled to the Africans the words of Revelation 7:14, of martyrs who washed their robes "white in the blood of the Lamb."

This exciting and well-written account provides a good look at how the New Testament had begun to influence Latin-as well as Greek-speaking Christians on martyrdom.

5. *Pionius*

This anonymous account dates *circa* 300, and its hero apparently died in the persecution of the emperor Decius (249-251). In Musurillo's words (p. xxviii), it is "artistically written" and includes "lengthy speaches of Pionius ... delivered to non-Christians as well as to Pionius' fellow Christians in prison." At this comparatively late date the canon of the New Testament was largely fixed, and most Christians were familiar with it. In Pionius' story, New Testament citations and motifs are not just present but are taken for granted.

Pionius has a vision of his suffering, and he accepts what must be. He does not refuse or avoid arrest. Unlike Jesus, who kept silent before his accusers, Pionius makes a speech, but it includes references to Matthew and 1 Peter. In response to a question, he cites John's gospel; in an exchange with a pagan temple official, he cites Acts and 1 Timothy. In prison he gives a speech to his fellow Christians and cites 2 Corinthians, Galatians, 1 John, Revelation, and Matthew, Mark, and Luke, which means that this account uses all four gospels. He also cites Acts which had been referred to earlier.

There is probably very little history in this account, but the biblical spirituality is there. Pionius, the martyr, the ideal Christian, stands in the tradition of the New Testament.

There are many more accounts of Christian martyrdoms, and although the amount of New Testament influence may vary, it is always there - except, of course, in the Roman court records which were prepared by pagans. Naturally Old Testament images also abound, especially those dealing with unjust suffering, such as the stories of Job or Daniel or Susanna (considered part of the Old Testament by the early Christians), and those dealing directly with martyrdom, such as 2 Maccabees (also considered canonical in the early Church). Some Christian accounts also reflect pagan folklore motifs. But, at base, martyrdom was the ultimate early Christian *imitatio Christi*, the imitation of Christ, and any understanding of martyrdom presupposed a knowledge of the New Testament.

B. Monasticism

The second great spiritual movement unique to the early Church is early monasticism. I stress "early monasticism" because although monasticism has been a feature of Christian life in every century since the third, only in the third, fourth, and fifth centuries do we find the primitive, heroic phase.

1. The Beginnings of Monasticism

No one can be sure exactly when Christian monasticism began. The traditional "first monk" is Antony of Egypt (ca. 251-356), who spent eighty years in the desert, but Athanasius, bishop of Alexandria, Antony's biographer - or, better, his hagiographer, that is, author of an edifying life of a saint - says that when Antony first left civilization for the desert he was advised by an older ascetic, so even the "Father of Monks" was not the first.

Why did Christians go to the desert? Scholars advance many theories, alone or in combination. Some see the distant influence of the Jewish Essenes or the community of Qumran on the Dead Sea; others see the influence of Greco-Roman philosophies which recommended withdrawal from the world and the exaltation of spiritual things. Closer to home, some scholars consider monasticism to be the logical extension of Christian teaching about the low value of worldly things and importance of renunciation. Since the monks often engaged in acts of self-denial or mortification (literally, to make dead), many scholars contend that the monks were the successors of the martyrs, that is, since persecutions require persecutors, when the persecutions ceased in the early fourth century, there were no more martyrs, no more of the ideal Christians of the early centuries. Into that void stepped the monks who died a little each day.

However it began, by the fourth century monasticism had become the ideal for many Christians. It attracted literally tens of thousands of the faithful to the deserts of the East or to the forests and offshore islands of the West. Many who could not practice monasticism completely introduced elements of monastic spirituality into their own lives, such as Jerome and his women counselees, or, if they were bishops, into the lives of their clergy, such as Ambrose or Augustine. A good number of fourth- and fifth-century bishops were ex-monks, the most prominent of these being Martin of Tours, John Chrysostom, and Nestorius.

The earliest monks practiced eremitic monasticism, that is, they lived as hermits. Of those who were completely hermits, we obviously know nothing. Of those hermits such as Antony, who were tracked down by would-be disciples, we have lives written by their disciples and admirers. Since there were many who wished to live lives of asceticism in the desert but could not endure the awesome psychological strain of a lifetime of solitude, another Egyptian, Pachomius (ca. 290-346), instituted cenobitic (from the Greek *koinos* - common and *bios* - life) monasticism, that is, communal monasticism. The Pachomian and other monastic communities regularly produced writings, such as rules, proverbs, prayers, and lives of famous Fathers or *abbas*. These writings quickly reached the outside world under such names as *The Sayings of the Fathers*. There were also accounts prepared by visitors to the monks or by monks who later left the desert; these include such important works as Athanasius' *Life of Saint Antony* and Palladius' *Lausiac History*. (All these works are readily available in English translation; consult the bibliography.) In these writings, intentionally and intensely spiritual, we can see the enormous influence of the New Testament on monastic spirituality and, indeed, on the understanding of monastic life.

2. Monastic Literature and the New Testament

The *Martyrdom of Saint Polycarp* dates *circa* 156; Athanasius' *Life of Saint Antony*, the first great treatise on the monks, dates to 357. In the two centuries separating these two works the New Testament had gone from a slowly forming corpus of Christian books to the new revealed word of God in a fixed canon. (Recall that Athanasius was the first one to name our twenty-seven books in his canon). All

Christians were supposed to live by the precepts of the New Testament, and the monastic literature contends that those precepts permeated the lives of the monks.

The basic life of the heroic monk - and only the lives of the successful ones survive - involved the renunciation of the secular world, the retreat to the desert, prayer and fasting, temptation by the devil and the successful overcoming of that temptation, miracle working, the instruction of disciples, and a blessed death. All these motifs derive from the life of Jesus. He retreated to the desert where the devil unsuccessfully tempted him (Matt 4:1-11, Mark 1:12-13, Luke 4:1-13). Throughout his public career Jesus worked miracles. He withdrew at times to pray (Luke 9:28-36; Matt 26:36), and he instructed his disciples. At the end of that career he died a blessed death.

Jesus was not the only role model for the monks. John the Baptist had retreated to the desert, the patriarch Abraham had left his home at God's call, and the prophet Elijah had to flee to the desert and the mountain because of his fearless ministry. The desert also had a great symbolic value as a sort of Garden of Eden, a world of nature to which the monks returned. But in general the monks saw Jesus himself as their model and guide.

In case the reader missed the rather unsubtle argument, the hagiographers routinely say that their heroes lived according to the Scriptures. When Antony speaks to his disciples about the spiritual life of the monk, he regularly refers to "the Scriptures" or "the gospels," and he cites a wide variety of biblical books, including especially the gospels of Matthew and Luke and the Pauline epistles. The fifth-century Greek monastic writer Palladius in his *Lausiac History* (chs. 34, 49) goes so far as to claim that among the monks particular scriptural passages were fufilled, and the ones he cites are 1 Cor 3:18 and Gal 3:28.

Sometimes the hagiographer worked the themes ingeniously. Athanasius tells of Antony's first retreat into the distant desert where he took up residence in an abandoned tomb, probably some pagan tomb which had been robbed (chs. 8-10). The devil and his minions attacked him constantly. After a particularly harsh encounter with them Antony saw a beam of light coming from heaven through the roof of his dwelling, and he felt his body to be more vigorous than it had been before, that is, he was resurrected into new life from his tomb.

Other elements of monastic spirituality, such as prayers and liturgies, were largely Christocentric and thus heavily centered on the New Testament, as they have been ever since.

Martyrdom and the monasticism of the desert are largely things of the past, but they are still vigorous reminders of how the New Testament dominated the spiritual life of the Early Christians.

II. Early Christian Art

A. Iconography

Iconography literally means "writing in images." In the twentieth century it has emerged as a major discipline in the study of religion and especially of Christianity. This interest derives from two factors, modern technology and modern theology.

Two elements of modern technology, travel and photography, have popularized iconography. Scholars had always studied Christian art, but modern modes of travel have enabled a great many people to see places like the catacombs, previously the preserve of the Romans and wealthy travellers. Photography has done far more. High-quality photographs, microfilms, and slides have enabled large numbers of people who do not travel to see the great works of Christian art, often better than they can be seen *in situ* because one does not have to peer around or over masses of tourists. Infra-red photography has even discovered aspects of Christian art not visible to the naked eye because some colors or lines had faded in the original. The easy availability of reproductions enables both scholar and lay person to study previously inaccessible treasures.

The modern theology which produced an interest in iconography is ecclesiology, that is, the study of the church. For generations many Roman Catholic theologians treated the Church as if it consisted primarily of the popes and bishops and only secondarily of everyone else. This attitude affected the study of church history because the history of the church was the history of the popes and bishops (and frequently the bishops were treated only in relation to the pope). On the other side, many Protestant theologians had a similarly narrow view. The Church for them was the church of the few, of the saved, of those set apart by grace from the rest of humanity.

Contemporary ecclesiology rightly rejects these constricted images and sees the Church including all of us, ordained and lay, saints and sinners, the whole People of God. The history of the Church is then the history of the People of God.

Here is where iconography plays a role. The Early Christian communities produced Early Christian art, and by studying that art we can tell something about the life of our Christians ancestors. This is hardly a foolproof method, but since the vast majority of Early Christians did not leave any writings behind, it is virtually the only way to study the community as a whole. It also provides a great help in determining approximately when the New Testament gained acceptance in the community.

B. The Earliest Art

We would naturally expect that the first Christian art would center on Christ, but it is a simple fact that we have no portrait of Jesus made from life or even from the memory of his disciples. The legend of Veronica's veil preserving the image of Christ's face does not appear until the fourteenth century, and although elements of it may be older, scholars give it no historical credence. As for the celebrated Shroud of Turin, its authenticity is vigorously debated, and while proponents of authenticity have frequently made strong arguments, the majority of scholars remain unconvinced. We must accept that at least for now we cannot be sure exactly what Jesus looked like.

Why not? Almost certainly because of the prohibition in Exodus 20:4 which forbade making images of God and the personified forces of the air, earth, and water. The Jews strictly enforced this prohibition, and when the Greek and Roman governors of Palestine tried to violate it by putting images of rulers in public places and even in the Temple, tense and often violent situations ensued. Jesus' first disciples were Jews, and they no doubt felt it religiously improper to produce images of Jesus.

When Christianity came to include large numbers of Gentiles, that is, by the early to mid-second century, there was less reluctance to make images, but by that time all those who knew Jesus personally were dead.

The first art was probably not art in the strict sense but rather simple symbols, such as the Chi-Rho (P, that is, Rho, with X, that is, Chi, through its stem). Clement of Alexandria, *circa* 200 asked those Christians who signed documents by placing their signet rings in soft wax to use for the symbols on their rings the dove (the Holy Spirit), the ship (of the Church), or the fish (the five Greek letters which spell "fish" are taken from the initial letters in the phrase "Jesus Christ, Son of God, Savior"), so we know that by the end of the second century symbols were widely used. A contemporary of Clement, the North African Tertullian, uses the fish as a symbol in his book on baptism, and he criticizes Christians who drink from glasses with the figure of the Good Shepherd embossed on them in gold.

Art as such appears first in the early third century in the Roman catacombs, the burial place for members of the local Christian community. (There are also pagan and Jewish catacombs.) Naturally the art reflects Christian beliefs about the afterlife, such as the orant, the deceased person standing with hands upraised in the form of prayer and/or rejoicing in salvation. Many Early Christians considered this life a trial to be endured on the way to eternal salvation, and not uncommonly the artistic motifs show Old Testament figures who had endured trial and triumphed. In times of persecution, this motif became even stronger as an encouragement to Christians to stand fast as their Jewish predecessors had done. The Old Testament figures included Noah, Job, Daniel in the lion's den, the three young men in the burning fiery furnace, and Susanna and the elders. These figures were simultaneously New Testament themes because they were types of Christ who endured unjust suffering.

The almost ideal type of Christ was Isaac, the only son who carried the promse but who had to carry the wood up the hill for his own sacrificial death. His last-second rescue by an angel provided a drama with much appeal for the ancient artists.

Without doubt the most popular Old Testament image was Jonah, whom the gospels identified as a type of Christ (Matt 12:39-41; Luke 11:29-32); indeed, some representations of Jonah may have their origins in the New Testament. Jonah, by being swallowed up by the sea-beast, had undergone a symbolic death since we all enter the belly of the earth, and then by emerging from the animal three days later he rose again as the Christ did and the Christians hoped they would do. Jonah fell asleep under a plant which grew miraculously; to the Early Christians this pointed to the Tree of Life in the Garden of Eden, a symbol of heaven; Jonah's sleep represented eternal rest.

C. New Testament Themes

But Christian art was one area in which interest in the Old Testament did not precede interest in the New. Contemporary with illustrations of Noah and Daniel were those of the Good Shepherd or the heavenly banquet, both New Testament images.

Pastoral themes were especially strong among the first Christians. Although the twenty-third psalm had described the Lord as a shepherd, the New Testament imagery was decisive. The shepherd is usually shown carrying the lamb on his shoulders, an image borrowed from pagan artistic themes and not from the Old Testament. Furthermore, it is one which corresponds to Luke 15:6: "And when he (the shepherd) has found it (the lost sheep), he lays it on his shoulders, rejoicing." This comes from the parable of the lost sheep (15:3-7) according to the gospel most likely written for Gentiles. It cannot be a coincidence that this detail is not found in the version of Matthew (18:12-14), the gospel most likely intended for a Jewish audience.

The image of Christ as the shepherd and the Christians as sheep reappears in John's gospel, primarily with Jesus' identification of himself as the Good Shepherd (10:1-18), the most important reference for Early Christians, but also in Jesus' charge to Peter, "Feed my lambs," "Feed my sheep" (21:15-17).

The Book of Revelation carried the pastoral image in a different direction, identifying Jesus not with the shepherd but with "the Lamb who was slain" (5:12) yet who triumphs over the forces of evil. This identification of Christ with those who suffered but triumphed would, like some of the Old Testament images, be especially pertinent in time of persecution.

The pictures of the celestial banquet warn us not to separate the images too strictly. For example, the image of a banquet in a place of tombs recalls the eschatological banquet, a strong theme of the gospels, for example, Matthew 8:11, "I tell you, many will come from east and west and sit at table with Abraham, Isaac, and Jacob in the kingdom of heaven," or the parable of the great supper (Matt 22:1-10, Luke 14:15-24), or Jesus' words at the Last Supper, "Truly, I say to you, I shall not drink again of the fruit of the vine until that day when I drink it new in the kingdom of God" (Mark 14:25).

Heaven as a place of plentiful food and drink would be a natural picture for the ancient people of Palestine who had to worry about poor harvests and food shortages. They pictured the Garden of Eden before the fall as a place where the man could "eat freely of every tree of the garden" (Gen 2:16), and they heard their Promised Land described as "a

"The Good Shepherd and his sheep," painted ceiling.

land flowing with milk and honey" (Exo 3:8). The gospel imagery grew out of the lived experience of the people.

But could even those Christians who knew the Old Testament background look at a picture of a banquet and not think of a contemporary eucharist? Probably not, nor would they be wrong in doing so because the eucharist had a strong relation to the sepulchral, that is, burial, imagery. The Christians believed death was a passage to a new life in Christ; the eucharist, a type of the eschatological banquet to be shared by all, brought this new life in Christ to those still alive. There was not in the third century a highly developed theology of the Real Presence, but the Christians certainly recognized the presence of Christ when they met in community (Matt 18:20) to share a eucharistic meal, and there was definitely some notion of his presence in the elements of the meal.

This likewise applies to the other great sacrament of Antiquity, baptism, the chief penitential sacrament of our earliest ancestors and one filled with images of death and rebirth, that is, that one died to a sinful life and rose again to a life in Christ. This view has a strong scriptural foundation, although it will suffice to cite but one passage, Romans 6:3-4: "Do you not know that all of us who have been baptized into Christ Jesus were baptized into his death? We were buried therefore with him by baptism into death, so that as Christ was raised from the dead by the glory of his Father, we too might walk in newness of life." This passage occurs in the most theologically important writing of the most important theologian of the apostolic age, and it was a work well-known to the Roman Christians who produced the catacomb frescoes, which included baptismal scenes and also Old Testament scenes which point to baptism, such as Noah and Jonah who both passed through water to a new life.

Another popular image but one unrelated to the Christian concepts of death and resurrection was that of the Magi coming to venerate Jesus. The gospel account (Matt 2:1-12) does not mention how many Magi there were, but since it mentions three gifts (2:11), Christian tradition has generally portrayed three magi. Possibly Gentile Christians favored themes which showed Jesus in contact with non-Jews. If that is so, the story of the Magi has special appeal since it tells of Gentiles who followed a star to worship Jesus while the king of the Jews tried to kill him. Further support for this theory can be found in the pictorial absence of the Jewish shepherds mentioned in Luke 2:8-20.

Baptismal Scene, Catacomb.

D. The Next Generations

Once the Christians had begun to express themselves artistically, they never turned back. By the mid-third century Christians using a house church at the town of Dura on the Euphrates River had decorated the house with frescoes, and Christian statuary survives from Rome and Syria. But the real changes occurred in the fourth century when the persecutions ceased and the Roman government patronized the Christians. Thanks to imperial commissions, magnificent churches arose in Rome and Constantinople with impressive and beautiful decorations for the interiors. Wealthy Christians commissioned sarcophagi, that is, stone tombs, ornamented with scenes from the Old and New Testaments. Manuscript Bibles had illuminations, as the illustrations are called, and Christian images appeared on personal jewelry. We can probably assume that in many private homes, including poor ones, simple, painted images could be found. Christian art had become a regular part of Christian life.

Not only did the Christian artists employ different media, but they also turned to a wide variety of biblical themes. The earliest artists had limited themselves to sepulchral and sacramental themes, but with the canon now virtually settled, the new generation of artists ranged all over the New Testament, often choosing what interested them personally or what interested their clients, but sometimes in response to particular conditions in the Church. For example, in the fourth century, when great controversies raged over the nature of the Trinity, the baptism of Christ became a favorite subject since it included Christ, the voice of the Father (who was often represented by a hand coming from a cloud), and the Holy Spirit in the form of dove. In the fifth century, when theologians were discussing how Mary was the mother of God, nativity scenes became popular.

Also popular were the apocrypha. Artists used apocryphal material to embellish New Testament scenes which they considered too meager. To cite the most obvious example, nativity scenes came to include the ox and the ass; the magi became three and acquired distinct ethnic backgrounds, that is, an Asiatic, an African, and a Caucasian; Joseph was portrayed as an elderly man (because of an apocryphal tale that he was a widower with grown children when he married Mary); and eventually a midwife joined the company.

Some of the apocrypha contained material widely considered heretical, but that did not stop the artists who usually used the non-controversial material, such as the wedding of Mary and Joseph. These themes persisted well into the Renaissance, and some are still common today.

Jesus heals the woman with the Hemorrage,
Catacomb.

The importance of Christian art for the acceptance and understanding of the New Testament cannot be underestimated. Visual images have an appeal that the written or spoken word usually cannot match, for example, in the modern world, the dominant role of television in carrying the news and the consequent decline in the number of daily newspapers. Many of the early faithful who could not read or who simply did not read the gospels saw pictures of Jesus' birth, public career, death, and resurrection; in the Early and Late Middle Ages, when the church was in a sorry state and clerical education and popular preaching had declined precipitously, these images, this iconography, continued to educate the people. Indeed, even in our scripture-conscious modern Christianity, it is likely that most people think that the Last Supper took place as Leonardo da Vinci painted it. Of course, in some cases, great artists offer insights into the accounts which scholars could not convey. Think of the stained-glass Life of Christ window at the French cathedral of Chartres which shows Jesus hanging on a green cross, that is, living wood to symbolize the cross as the Tree of Life. Or consider the great psychological power of Rembrandt's "Supper at Emmaus" with its brilliant use of darkness and light to demonstrate the effect of Jesus upon those at table with him. We shudder to think what might have been lost if the Christians had refrained from making images.

We began this book by noting how much we take for granted about the New Testament - the name, the books, the text - and for which we must thank the Early Church. While we may value the pictorial representation of New Testament scenes less than we value these others, it definitely played a key role in gaining a place for the New Testament among the Early Christians, and it is a precious heritage from our earliest ancestors in the Faith.

BIBLIOGRAPHY

CHAPTER 1

Robert M. Grant, *The Formation of the New Testament* (New York 1965).

Joseph F. T. Kelly, editor, *Perspectives on Scripture and Tradition* (Notre Dame, Indiana, 1976).

C.F.D. Moule, "How the New Testament Came into Being," in *Understanding the New Testament*, edited by O. Jessie Lace, *Cambridge Bible Commentary* (New York, 1965).

Robert L. Wilken, *The Myth of Christian Beginnings* (Garden City, New York, 1971).

CHAPTERS 2-3

There is a mountain of books on the New Testament. This is a list of the ones I used for these chapters; it is not at all meant to be a basic New Testament bibliography.

A good general introduction is *Introduction to the New Testament* by Werner Kümmel (Abingdon, Tennessee, 1975).

The one-volume commentary, *The Jerome Biblical Commentary*, edited be Raymond Brown, Joseph Fitzmyer, and Roland E. Murphy (Englewood Cliffs, New Jersey, 1968), is aging a bit but of great value.

There are many series of individual commentaries. I consulted *The Cambridge Bible Commentary* (New York) and *The Anchor Bible* (Garden City, N.Y.). The general reader is advised to consult the *New Testament Message*, edited by Wilfrid Harrington and Donald Senior for Michael Glazier, Inc., for readable and up-to-date introductions and commentaries.

Individual volumes also consulted for these chapters include:

S.G.F. Brandon, *The Fall of Jerusalem and the Christian Church* (London, 1951).

Raymond Brown, *The Community of the Beloved Disciple* (New York, 1979).

Raymond Brown and John Meier, *Antioch and Rome* (New York, 1983).

Benedict Hegarty, "Chloe to Paul," in *Sowing the Word*, edited by Patrick Rogers (Dublin, 1983), pp. 225-230.

CHAPTER 4

Translations of patristic works can be found in the series *Fathers of the Church* (Washington) and *Ancient Christian Writers* (Washington).

Of great value for this chapter were *The Apostolic Fathers* in the *Fathers of the Church* series, translated by Francis X. Glimm *et al.*, and Eusebius' *History of the Church*, translated by G. A. Williamson (Baltimore, 1965).

Collections of individual tests can be found in *A New Eusebius*, edited by James Stevenson (London, 1974), *Second-Century Christianity: A Collection of Fragments*, edited by Robert M. Grant (London, 1957), and *Documents in Early Christian Thought*, edited by Maurice Wiles and Mark Santer (New York, 1975), which provided the translation for the excerpts from Irenaeus.

Introductions to the New Testament and one-volume commentaries usually have chapters on the canon.

Individual studies used for this chapter include:
Kurt Aland, *The Problem of the New Testament Canon (London, 1962)*.

William Farmer and Denis Farkasfalvy, The *Formation of the New Testament Canon* (New York, 1983).

John Knox, *Philemon among the Epistles of Paul* (Abingdon, 1959).

Hans von Campenhausen, *Ecclesiastical Authority and Spiritual Power in the Church of the First Three Centuries* (Stanford, California, 1969).

Hans von Campenhausen, *The Formation of the Christian Bible* (Philadelphia, 1972).

CHAPTER 5

There are two basic English translations of the New Testament apocryphal literature. The better is *New Testament Apocrypha*, edited by Edgar Hennecke and revised by Wilhelm Schneelmelcher (Philadelphia, 1963-66), 2 vols, with valuable introductory essays. The second is *The Apocryphal New Testament*, edited by M. R. James (Oxford, 1924; repr. 1975).

Many Gnostic apocrypha are available in *The Nag Hammadi Library in English*, edited by James M. Robinson (New York, 1978).

Individual studies cited in the chapter are:
Jean Danielou, *The Theology of Jewish Christianity* (Chicago, 1964).

Robert M. Grant, "The Description of Paul in the Acts of Paul and Thecla," *Vigiliae Christianae* 36 (1982), 1-4.

Elaine Pagels, *The Gnostic Gospels* (New York, 1979).

CHAPTERS 6-7

Articles on the text and versions of the New Testament can be found in New Testament introductions and one-volume commentaries.

There are also many good articles in *The Cambridge History of the Bible*, edited by P. R. Ackroyd, *et. al.* (New York, 1963-1971), 3 volumes:

from volume one-

Matthew Black, "The Biblical Languages," 1-11;

C. H. Roberts, "Books in the Graeco-Roman World and in the New Testament," 48-66;

J. N. Birdsall, "The New Testament Text," 308-377.

from volume two-

T. C. Skeat, "Early Christian Book Production: Papyri and Manuscripts," 54-79;

Raphael Loewe, "The Medieval History of the Latin Vulgate," 102-154;

M. J. Hunter, "The Gothic Bible," 338-362.

Geoffrey Shepherd, "English Versions of the Scriptures before Wycliffe," 362-387.

These individual studies were basic for these chapters:
Jack Finegan, *Encountering New Testament Manuscripts* (Grand Rapids, Michigan, 1974).

Bruce Metzger, *The Early Versions of the New Testament* (Oxford, 1977).

Bruce Metzger, *The Text of the New Testament* (Oxford, 1964).

CHAPTER 8

For accounts of the martyrs, the best book is *The Acts of the Christian Martyrs*, edited by Herbert Musurillo (Oxford, 1972). *The Life of Saint Antony* by Athanasius and *The Lausiac History* by Palladius, both translated by Robert Meyer, are in volumes 10 and 34 of *Ancient Christian Writers*. In *Western Asceticism*, edited by Owen Chadwick (Philadelphia, 1958), is a translation of *The Sayings of the Fathers*.

These individual studies were consulted for this chapter:
Louis Bouyer, *The Spirituality of the New Testament and the Fathers* (New York, 1963).

Derwas Chitty, *The Desert a City* (Oxford, 1966).

W. H. C. Frend, *Martyrdom and Persecution in the Early Church* (Oxford, 1965).

Andre Grabar, *Christian Iconography* (Princeton, 1968).

Walter Lowrie, *Art in the Early Church* (New York, 1969).

GLOSSARY

ALLEGORY — an account given on one level but with its meaning on a higher level.

APOCALYPTIC — a Jewish literary genre in which a seer has visions, usually about cataclysmic divine intervention in the world to right wrongs.

APOCRYPHON, APOCRYPHA — literally, "hidden" books, but commonly those books which were candidates for the canon or which claim to be by or about biblical figures.

APOLOGIST — one who defends a position with rational arguments.

APOSTOLICITY — the notion that all authentic Christian teaching must go back to the apostles or at least be consonant with their teachings.

ASCETICISM — bodily self-denial for a spiritual good.

CANON — 1) the list of biblical books and 2) the rationale behind such a list.

CHRISTOLOGY — the theology of Christ, usually centering on who he is and what is his role in the economy of salvation.

CODEX — a book consisting of pages placed together and bound together at one end.

CORPUS — Latin word for 'body,' here meaning a body of literature.

DIAKONOS — Greek word for 'one who serves,' origin of the Christian word 'deacon'.

DOCETISM — the belief that Christ did not have a body but only seemed to have one.

ECCLESIOLOGY — the theology of the Church.

EPISKOPOS — Greek word for 'overseer;' it came to mean 'bishop'.

ESCHATOLOGY — the theology of the last things, the end of the world.

EVANGELIST — a writer of a gospel; sometimes used of missionaries.

EXEGESIS — the study of the biblical text to determine the author's meaning.

FUNDAMENTALIST — an occasionally inexact word but usually used of someone who takes most narrative passages of the Bible to be historical.

GNOSTIC — a wide-ranging term, but generally meaning someone who claimed to have a special knowledge (Greek: *gnosis*) of the cosmos or of some secret teaching of Jesus or his immediate disciples.

HAGIOGRAPHY — the written life of a saint, usually intended to edify the reader.

HETERODOX — something at variance with orthodox teaching.

ICONOGRAPHY — literally, to write in images; commonly, to convey a message via the visual arts.

LOCUS — Latin word for 'place,' used in theology of a source for a particular teaching.

LOGOS — Greek word for 'word,' used of Jesus in John's gospel and in Revelation.

MANUSCRIPT — a book written by hand.

PAPYRUS — a plant growing along the banks of the Nile and used in the ancient world for writing material.

PAROUSIA — the Second Coming of Jesus.

PATRISTIC — applying to the Fathers of the Church, for example, patristic theology.

PHILOLOGY — the study of words and how they are used in languages.

PRESBYTEROS — Greek word for 'elder,' came to mean 'priest'.

PSEUDEPIGRAPHA — writings for which the author used a false name (pseudonym).

QUMRAN — a settlement on the Dead See where the famous scrolls were found.

ROLL — a book consisting of pages sewn together into one long strip which was then 'rolled' onto two thick wooden bars and unrolled when one wished to read.

SCRIBE — a professional copyist of manuscripts.

SEPTUAGINT — a Greek version of much of the Hebrew Bible, prepared by Jews living outside Palestine.

SYNOPTIC — literally, "to see together," a term applied to the gospels of Matthew, Mark, and Luke because of their similarities.

TEXTUAL CRITICISM — the scholarly discipline which attempts to reconstruct the original wording or text of a written work, especially an ancient one.

TYPOLOGY — for ancient Christians, the notion that events or persons in the Hebrew Bible pointed to events or persons in the New Testament.

INDEX

Abgar V, 110-111, 145.
Abraham, 174, 179.
Acts of the Apostles, 19-20, 23, 24-26, 29, 32, 34, 36, 38, 42, 45, 56, 64-67, 70-71, 82, 95, 100-101, 106, 109, 113, 115, 127, 141, 142, 145, 146, 148, 153, 161, 163, 166-167, 169, 170-171.
Acts of Paul, 113, 115.
Acts of Peter, 112-113, 115.
Acts of Pilate, 110.
Acts of Thomas, 115.
Adam, 110, 142.
Adiabene, royal house of, 145.
Ahimelech, 50.
Alexander the Great, 141.
Alexandria, 24-25, 28, 99, 100-101, 115, 130, 135-136, 147-150, 153, 172.
Alfred the Great, 163.
Alogi, 97.
Alphabet, Cyrillic, 162.
Alphabet, Glagolitic, 162.
Alphabet, Slavonic, 162.
Ambrose, 78, 173.
Amphilochius of Iconium, 101.
Anna, 105, 109, 146.
Antioch, 25, 27, 39, 47-48, 82-83, 100, 145.
Antiochene School, 164.
Antony, 148, 172, 174-175.
Apocalypse, Book of - see Revelation.
Apocalypse of Paul, 117.
Apocalypse of Peter, 98, 103, 116, 117.
Apocrypha, 103-114, 183.
    acts, 112-116.
    apocalypses, 116-117.
    epistles, 111-112.
    gospels, 107-111.
    and canon, 117-119.

Apocryphon of John, 108-109.
Apologetics, 86.
Apollos, 148.
Apologists, 86.
Arabia, 152-153.
Aramaic, 48, 142.
Arianism, 160-161.
Aristeas, Letter of, 28.
Armenia, 149-151.
Art, 164-185.
Ascension, 65.
Asia Minor, 52, 55, 57, 59, 63, 85, 87, 89, 92, 97, 113, 125, 147, 150, 160, 168.
Athanasius, 101, 153, 172-175.
Augustine, 41, 78, 102, 156, 173.

Babylon, 24-25, 57, 63.
Baptism, 181.
Barnabas, 26, 30, 36, 45, 85, 100-101, 112, 141.
Barnabus Justus, 115.
Bardesanes, 145.
Barnabas, Epistle of, 78, 85, 98, 148.
Barth, Karl, 30.
Bartholomew, 149, 153.
2 Baruch, 62, 85, 89.
3 Baruch, 62, 85, 89.
Basil the Great, 78.
Basilides, 83, 107.
Bede, 163.
Beloved Disciple, 53, 75.
Berber dialects, 155.
Bishop (episkopos), 82-83, 94.
Blandina, 169.
Bohairic, 148.
Buddha, 22.
Byzantine, 135-136, 151, 153-154, 162.

Caedmon, 163.
Caesarea (Palestine), 99-101.
Calvin, John, 155.
Canon, 68-102.
Cappadocia, 160.
Carthage, 102, 155.
Cassiodorus, 158.
Catacombs, Roman, 177, 184.
Catholic Epistles, 15, 57, 60, 63, 95-96, 101, 146, 161.
Catullus, 132.
Ceolfrith, 158.
Cerinthus, 97.
Charisius, 116.
Chi-Rho, 177.
Chloe, 31.
Christology, 44, 53-54.
Christos, 25.
Church, Slavonic, 162.
Claudius (emperor), 145.
Clement of Alexandria, 42, 61, 98-99, 105, 114, 177.
Clement of Rome, 30, 78, 80-81, 83, 85, 95-96, 98, 100, 104, 118, 142, 148.
2 Clement, 85.
Codex (Caudex), 127, 129.
Codex Amiatinus, 158-159.
Codex Argenteus, 161.
Codex Sinaiticus, 131.
Colossians, 29, 33, 42, 45, 57-58, 72-73, 81, 84, 89, 97, 104, 111.
Confucius, 22.
Constantine, 34, 130, 162.
Constantinople, 160-161, 182.
Coptic, 147-149.
Corinth, 19, 31, 32, 80.
1 Corinthians, 17, 19, 29, 31-33, 43, 48, 65, 70-71, 72, 76, 78, 80-81, 84, 89, 97, 170, 174.
2 Corinthians, 17, 29, 30, 31-33, 70, 72, 78, 84-85, 89, 114, 117, 167, 169, 171.
3 Corinthians, 114.
Corinthians, apocryphal letter of, 151.
Cornelius, 24, 66.
Cyprian, 156.
Cyril of Jerusalem, 101.
Cyril, 162.

Da Vinci, Leonardo, 185.
Damasus I, Pope, 157.
Daniel, Book of, 62, 171.
David, 110.

Dead Sea Scrolls, 139.
Decius, emperor, 148, 170.
Diakonoi, 82, 156.
Dialogue with Trypho, 86.
Diatessaron, 145-146, 157, 163.
Didache, 85, 98, 100.
Diognetus, 30.
Dionysius of Alexandria, 100, 149.
Dionysius, of Corinth, 142.
Diotrephes, 57.
Docetists, 82-83.
Douay-Rheims, 120.
Domitian, 63.
Dura, 182.

Eadfrid, Bishop of Lindisfarne, 163.
Ebionites, 107.
Edessa, Church of, 21, 105.
Egypt, 61, 77, 100, 107-110, 116, 122, 126, 147-149, 153-154.
Elijah, 46, 110, 174.
Encratites, 145.
1 Enoch, 62, 76.
2 Enoch, 62.
Epaphroditus, 45.
Epaphras, 33.
Ephesus, 52, 81-82, 84, 114.
Ephesians, 29, 33, 60-61, 72, 73, 81, 84, 89, 97, 104.
Epiphanius of Salamis, 109.
Epistles, 56-62.
    see Barnabas, Epistle of
        Peter, Epistle of
        James, Epistle of
        John, Epistle of
        Jude, Epistle of
        Ephesians, Epistle of
        Hebrews, Epistle of
Epistles, Apocryphal, 111-112.
Erasmus, 134.
Eschatology, 22.
Esdras, Book of, 85.
Essenes, 172.
Esther, Book of 75.
Ethiopia, 153-154.
Euphrates, 182.
Eusebius, 24, 37, 61, 88, 90, 91, 100-101, 115, 142, 148-149, 150, 161, 169.
Euthymius, 151.
Exodus, 50, 177, 180.
Ezana, King, 153.
4 Ezra, 62.

Fayyumic, 148.
Festus, 66.
Frumentius, 153.

Gaius (of Rome), 57, 97.
Galatians, 17, 29, 31, 70, 80-81, 84, 88, 97, 169, 171, 174.
Ge'ez, 153.
Genesis, 59.
Gnosticism, 30, 43, 53, 77, 83, 91-93, 95, 97, 100, 107-108, 109, 116, 118.
and apostolicity, 91-92.
Good Samaritian, 46.
Gospel According to the Egyptians, 98.
Gospel According to the Hebrews, 98.
Gospel of Nicodemus, 110.
Gospel of Thomas, 104.
Gospels, The, 38-55, 74-75.
see Matthew
Mark
Luke
John
Gospels, Apocryphal 107-111.
Goths, 160-162.
Graphe, 77, 85, 94-95.
Greece, 45, 99.
Gregory I the Great, 158.
Gregory the Illuminator, 150.
Gundophorus, 115.

Hadrian II, Pope, 162.
Hebrews, (Book of), 17, 50, 61-62, 76, 80, 84, 96, 98, 100-102, 148, 161, 166, 169.
Hellenism, 23, 25, 82, 99, 141, 147.
Herod, 49.
Herod Agrippa, 66-67.
Hermas, 77.
Hermas, Shepherd of, 77, 95, 98, 100-101, 116, 142.
Herodotus, 127.
Hieracas, 148.
Hilary of Poitiers, 102.
Hippolytus, 98.
Homer, 28.
"Hymn of the Pearl," 115-116.

Iberia, Kingdom of, 151.
Iconography, 175-176.
Iconium, 113-114.
Ignatius of Antioch, 30, 81-84, 96, 142, 167.

India, 115.
Infancy narratives, 49-50, 105.
Irenaeus, 87, 92-96, 98, 100, 105, 114, 118.
Isaiah, 42, 64, 76, 115.
Isaac, 179.

Jacob, 76, 179.
Jacobites, 147.
James, 15, 17, 22, 57-59, 78, 98, 100-102, 104, 166, 169.
Jamnia, 75.
Jeremiah, 17.
Jerome, 111, 157-158, 160, 172-173.
Jerusalem Bible, 18.
Jerusalem Church, 25, 36-37.
Jewish War (of 66-70), 28.
Joachim, 105, 109.
Job, 178.
Joel, 26, 62.
1 John, 15, 56, 84, 95, 96, 97, 98, 100, 101, 170, 171.
2 John, 15, 18, 56, 84, 95, 98, 100, 101, 147.
3 John, 15, 18, 56, 57, 82, 100, 101, 147.
John the Baptist, 109-110, 174.
John Chrysostom, 78, 101, 173.
John VIII, 162.
John of Ephesus, (monophysite historian) 154.
Jonah, 178, 181.
Josephus, 36.
Jude, 15, 17, 22, 59, 76-77, 97-98, 101-103, 147, 168.
Judas, 168.
Julius Caesar, 41.
Justin Martyr, 77, 86-87, 105, 114, 142. 145.
Justinian, emperor, 154.

Kells, Book of, 149.
King James (version of Bible), 121, 143.
1 Kings, 153, 161.
Knox, John, 84.

Lamentations, Book of, 75.
Laodicea, 33, 72, 89, 111.
Lao-Tse, 22.
Laurentian Library, 158.
Lausiac History, 173-174.
Lazarus, 46, 110.

Lectionaries, 130-132.
Lindisfarne Gospels, 163.
Logos, 97.
Lucian of Antioch, 100-101.
Lucifer of Cagliari, 102.
Luke, 15, 17, 21, 25, 29, 36, 40-41, 45-47,
    49, 50, 62, 64, 65, 70-71, 74-75, 76, 80,
    81-82, 86, 88, 94-96, 97, 106-107, 127,
    129, 130, 138-139, 142, 146, 157, 161,
    166, 167, 169, 170, 171, 174, 178, 179,
    181.
Luther, Martin, 30, 89, 102, 143, 155.
Lyons, 168, 170.

1 Maccabees, 141.
2 Maccabees, 141, 171.
MacRegol gospels, 163.
Manassah, 76.
Magnesia, 81, 83.
Mani, 22, 107.
Marcion, 87-88, 91, 93, 97, 104, 157.
Marcus Aurelius, 168.
Mariology, 109.
Mark, 15, 21, 22, 36, 42-45, 46, 48, 50, 62,
    70-71, 74, 81, 86, 94-97, 129, 138, 142,
    146, 151, 157, 166, 170, 171, 174, 179.
Martin of Tours, 173.
Martyrdom, 165-167.
"Martyrdom of St. Polycarp," 168-169,
    173.
Mary, 105, 109, 144, 183.
Mary Magdalene, 107-108, 109.
Mary, Gospel of, 108.
Matthew, 15, 36, 40-41, 46-47, 48-52, 62,
    70-71, 74-75, 80, 81, 84-86, 94, 97, 104,
    106, 115, 120, 129, 138, 146, 153, 157,
    162, 166, 168, 169, 171, 174, 178, 179,
    181.
Matthew, Aramaic, 48.
Maximilla, 89, 90.
Melito of Sardis, 88.
Menelik, 153.
Mesrop, 150-151.
Methodius of Olympus, 116, 162.
Minuscule, 130-132, 134-135.
Misdaeus, King, 116.
Missionaries, 24-25, 28-29.
Monasticism, 171-175.
Monophysites, 147, 153-154.
Montanus, 89-93.
Montanists, 169.
Moses, 76.

Muratorian fragment, 96, 116, 156.
Muratori, Ludovico, 96.
Mygdonia, 116.

Nag Hammadi, 77.
"The Harrowing of Hell," 110.
Nero, 34-35, 37, 63, 66.
Nestorius, 152, 173.
New American Bible, 121.
New English Bible, 18.
New Testament,
    composition of, 21-67.
Nicodemus, 107.
Nine Saints, 153.
Nino, 151.
Noah, 178, 181.
North Africa, 90, 155, 165, 169.
Novatian, 156.
Nubia, 154.

Old Latin (Vetus Latina), 156.
Onesimus, 33, 84.
Oral tradition, 41, 44-45, 74, 81, 85, 97.
Origen, 61, 99-100, 114, 148, 152, 164.

Pachomius, 148, 149, 173.
Palladius, 173-174.
Pantaenus, 115, 148.
Papa, 152.
Papias, 42, 44, 48, 52.
Papyrus, 30, 127-132, 148.
Parousia, 31, 58, 60, 62, 67.
Palimpsests, 161.
"Passion of Saints Perpetua and Felicity"
    169.
Passion narrative, 40.
Pastorals, 55-56.
Patristics, 78-80.
Paul, 15, 21, 23-37, 38-46, 55-56, 59-62,
    64-67, 70-77, 80-84, 86-87, 88-89, 91,
    94-102, 104, 106, 111-119, 121, 122,
    128-129, 141, 144-145, 156, 166, 167,
Pelagius, 89.
Pella, 37.
Pepuza, 89-90.
Pergamon, 125.
Perpetua, 170.
Persecution, Neronian, 34-36.
Persia, 150, 152.
Peshitta, (Syriac New Testament) 146-
    147, 152.
1 Peter, 15, 22-23, 36, 59-60, 78, 81, 84,

95, 96, 100-101, 104, 110, 112, 142, 169, 171.
2 Peter, 16-17, 22, 42, 59, 72, 76-77, 78, 83, 98, 100-101, 104, 142, 147, 169.
Pharisees, 21, 46, 49, 50-52, 65.
Philadelphia, 81-82.
Philae, 154.
Philemon, 29, 33, 42, 43, 45, 61, 72, 84, 89, 95, 97, 98, 100.
Philippi, 114.
Philippians, 29, 33, 77, 80, 81, 84-85, 89, 97, 100.
Philomelium, Church of, 168.
Philoxenus, Bishop of Mabbug, 147.
Phoenicia, 25.
Phrygia, 89.
Pionius, 170-171.
Pius, (Bishop of Rome), 97.
Plato, 124, 132.
Pliny the Younger, 63.
Polycarp of Smyrna, 30, 63, 77, 81, 84-85, 92, 94-95, 147, 167-168, 170.
Pontus, 87.
"Preaching of Peter," 98.
Presbyters (presbyteroi), 58, 63, 83.
Priscilla, 89-90.
Protoevangelium of James, 105, 109.
Psalms, 26, 75, 148, 158.
"Pseudo-Clementine Recognition," 118.
Ptolemy, 30.

Quadratus, 78.
"Queen of the Versions," 151.
Quelle source, 40-41, 46.
"The Questions of Mary," 109.
Qumran, 22, 76, 172.

Rembrandt, 185.
Rabbula, Bishop of Edessa, 147.
Revelation, Book of, 17-18, 30, 52, 57, 62-64, 95-96, 100-103, 112, 127, 137, 145, 146-147, 151, 161, 166, 168, 170-171, 179.
    see also Apocalypse, Book of
    Revised Standard Version, 18, 120.
Romans, 17, 29, 32, 33, 59, 70-71, 80-81, 84, 89, 97, 122, 128, 142, 169, 170, 181.
Rome, 25, 32, 33, 34, 36, 57, 60, 63, 64, 66, 67, 80, 81, 83, 87, 88, 92, 94, 97, 106, 111, 112, 113, 114, 115, 135, 142, 145, 158, 165, 168, 182.
Ruth, Book of, 75.

Sahac, 150.
Sahidic, 148.
Samaritans, 23, 54.
Samaria, 24-25.
1 Samuel, 50.
Saturus, 170.
"Sayings of the Fathers," 147, 173.
Scillitan Martyrs, 155.
Second Vatican Council, 154-155.
Seneca, 111.
Septuagint, 28, 80, 141, 157-158.
Sermon on the Mount, 50.
Seth, 110.
Sheba, Queen of, 153.
Shem'on, Bishop, 152.
Shapur II (King), 152.
Shroud of Turin, 176.
Sibyl, 28.
Sibylline Oracles, 62.
Sibylline books, 28.
Silvanus, 23, 30.
Simeon, 46.
Simon Magus, 112.
Simon of Cyrene, 83.
Socrates, 22.
Sogdian, 152.
Solomon, 153.
Song of Songs, 75.
Sosthenes, 31.
Soter, Pope, 142.
Spain, 32.
Spirituality, 165-175.
Smyrna, 81-84, 92, 94.
Stemma, 134-135.
Stephen, 166.
Stichometry, 129.
Succession, apostolic, 94.
Susanna, 171, 178.
Syria, 43, 97, 100, 101, 107, 109-110, 118, 145, 146, 147, 182.

Tacitus, 34.
Tatian, (the Syrian) 86, 145, 146, 157, 163.
Teacher of Righteousness, 22.
Tertius, 128.
Tertullian, 77, 87, 90, 98, 113, 114, 156, 166, 177.
Testament of the Twelve Patriarchs, 62.
Textual criticism, 120-140.
Thaddeus, 145, 149.
Theodora (empress), 154.
Theodoret, Bishop of Cyrrhus, 147.

Thecla, 113-114.
Theophrastus, 127.
Theophilus, 45, 64.
1 Thessalonians 22, 23, 29, 30, 33, 65, 71, 81, 84, 89, 97, 101, 122, 166.
2 Thessalonians, 104, 166.
Thomas, Gospel of, 101, 109.
1 Timothy, 29, 30, 31, 55, 56-57, 84, 97, 101, 169-170.
2 Timothy, 16, 29, 42, 45, 55, 56, 84.
Tiridates, 150.
Titus, 29, 55, 56, 97.
Tralles, 81-83.
Translations, Arabic, 154.
Translations, Armenian, 142-144, 151.
Translations, Gothic, 142-144, 160.
Translations, Latin, 142-144.

Translations, Syriac, 142-144, 151, 154.
Trinity, 78, 160, 161.
Tyre, 153.

Unicals, 130-132, 134-135.
Ulfilas, 160, 161.

Victor I, Pope, 155.
"Vision of Paul," 104.
Vulgate (Vulgata Latina), 156, 158, 160.

Wisdom of Solomon, 97.
Wycliffe, John, 163.

Zacharias, 109.
Zoroaster, 22.